BUYING

AMERICA

THE RIGHT WAY

**What overseas real estate investors
need to know to get it right
when buying in America**

*FOREWORD BY THAN MERRILL
OF FORTUNEBUILDERS*

BY FRANK J. YACENDA

Copyright Notice

Disclaimer

The purpose of this book is to provide general information to overseas real estate investors on setting up their investment vehicles and doing business in the U.S. Since each situation is different and unique, questions specific to individual circumstances should be addressed to an appropriate professional. The author and the publisher specifically disclaim any liability or loss incurred as a direct or indirect result of using, applying, or relying on any of the information or approaches contained in this book.

Dedication

This book is dedicated to all my great overseas clients who have shown me how much there is a need for this book. It is hard to imagine a group of more pleasant, responsive, and supportive people anywhere, and I am forever in their debt. I hope this book is but one small way of re-paying that debt to them, and others who will follow.

Table of Contents

Foreword

At FortuneBuilders, we stress that the more you learn, the more you earn. In **Buying America the Right Way**, Frank Yacenda helps overseas investors learn not just the basic ins and outs of doing business in the U.S., but also the potential pitfalls they face. Thus, investors learn how to set up their businesses both to optimize income while protecting their earnings.

Geared specifically toward real estate investors, Frank offers sound advice – of equal utility to American investors – on how to protect against litigious tenants, unscrupulous and incompetent property managers, and the tax collector. He also shares FortuneBuilders' philosophy that it's not how much money you take in, but how much you get to keep at the end that counts most. With that principle in mind, he offers strategies and techniques that work for both smaller and larger investors.

Many of Frank's clients say they wish they had this book before they invested in the U.S. Indeed, venturing into new territory without a guide can be puzzling, stressful, and costly. Frank responded to these concerns, and this book is the local guide that, concisely and clearly, explains the lay of the land and leads the reader through each step of the way, both in the main text and in extensive FAQs. While he urges readers to consult knowledgeable advisers on key issues, he offers ways they can save on what they pay out to consultants.

Investing in real estate in the U.S. can be a profitable and satisfying activity, and one that offers the potential for both significant gains and long-term income to the informed investor. Doing things the right way is the surest route to profitable and successful investment, and that's precisely what this book is about.

Than Merrill
Founder and CEO of
FortuneBuilders

Introduction

This book is intended for the overseas investor investing in real estate in the United States, but it can be of equal utility to the American investor. There is so much information, misinformation, confusion, and doubt out there, both groups of investors can benefit from a concise guide to setting up a suitable investment structure and the essential ins and outs of doing business in the U.S. And that's what this is.

The basic assumption of this guide is that the investor will choose to operate through, and own properties in the name of, limited-liability entities – limited liability companies (LLCs), corporations, and related business forms. While these entity forms would not normally apply to ownership of one's own private residence, they are the vehicles of choice for real estate investors seeking to protect their assets and limit personal liability associated with their investment properties and activities. It is said that the United States is a litigious society, and this factor should not be underestimated. Unlike what you may or may not be used to in your home country, this is a key factor advising the overseas investor to operate in the U.S. through a limited liability entity.

I also assume that most smaller investors don't have endless resources to expend on legal, accounting, corporate, or tax advice. Knowledge of some basic tenets and guidelines can go a long way toward understanding the framework within which one will be operating.

That is a good starting point, and will help control consultant costs, but each situation has its specific questions, differences, and fine points.

Things can be especially tricky in the area of taxation, with federal and usually state tax filings required in the U.S., and other tax filings required in the investor's home jurisdiction. Add on the complexity of such things as bilateral investor or trader treaties, special investment vehicles, such as retirement funds, and different ways of structuring investment holdings, and there are any number of mines that the unwary can step onto unwittingly.

While I hope this guide serves as a good starting point, I strongly urge the budding investor (and even those past the "budding" stage) to seek out competent professional advice as deemed necessary, particularly in the areas of accounting and taxation. And do look for those professionals familiar with both U.S. tax and accounting law and practice as well as that of your home country.

I want to make a disclaimer right at the outset, which is that I am not an attorney, accountant, tax, or investment adviser. While I have made great effort to be develop and present information that is as accurate as possible at the time of publication, I cannot, and do not, warrant that it is without fault or that different guidance, advice, or interpretation might not apply to any given situation. Law and regulation are also continually changing, so what is correct today may not be tomorrow.

Additionally, I cannot give you definitive guidance or advice in legal, accounting, tax, or investment matters as it pertains to your particular situation, and you are specifically advised to seek out professional advice in those areas before proceeding with any investment. My primary role is processing documents for investors seeking to set up U.S. companies, not in serving as an investment, accounting, tax, or legal adviser.

I will set up whatever company or structure a client wishes, and when I see them, I will point out any obvious issues or problems, but beyond that you should obtain competent professional advice prior to making key investment or structural decisions.

One last caveat on this matter. Always keep in mind that it is not how much money your investments bring in. It is how much you get to keep that matters. There are plenty of sharks out there who will be happy to take your money, smiling all the way to the bank. That does not say not to use consultants and advisers. It says to select them carefully, and to use them judiciously, keeping a cost-benefit analysis always in mind.

The intent of this guide is to help you minimize, not eliminate, your consultant costs, and to give you a good grounding in what things to be aware of, both in selecting and using consultants and in structuring and pursuing your investments.

In line with this principle – that it is not how much you bring in, it is how much you keep – my philosophical approach is to keep things as simple as possible and still accomplish what you need to.

Most smaller investors are not going to need the same level of complexity to protect their downside that a major corporate investor might require. In the course of this guide I offer approaches of varying levels of complexity. I also note alternatives that investors can consider to achieve their ends. It is up to you to decide which levels of complexity, and which alternatives, work for you in any given circumstance, and to keep that cost-benefit analysis always in mind.

Note that the guidance offered in this book can be as applicable whether you are acquiring properties to flip, buy and hold, or even to serve as a vacation home for you that also can generate income.

I hope you find the reading clear and enjoyable, and that this guide helps clear much of the fog from your path. I have organized it in the general order of steps and issues you will need to concern yourself with. All are important and should be incorporated in your planning, but the order in which you'll deal with them roughly parallels the order in which they are presented in this guide.

I think, whatever you do, it should be fun, and I'll try to keep things that way for you in this guide. I would be happy to hear from you with both positive and less-than-positive comments and critiques. And I would be most pleased to assist you and your colleagues and associates in setting up your U.S. investment structures and vehicles.

Happy reading, and even happier investing!

Basics and Objectives

Any worthwhile undertaking asks that you set out your objectives at the outset. These objectives will guide your decisions and actions as you go along and will help you evaluate if you are on course, beginning to go off-course, or badly off-course, and what course corrections might be required.

It's said that when you don't know where you're going any road will get you there, and that is certainly true in the realm of investing. And it's a great way to wind up in serious trouble, lose money, and probably become disillusioned with your investments. I've seen it happen all too often, and I've seen it happen that people will blame others for their mishaps when the root cause is failure on their part to take necessary steps and to keep a close eye on their investments and incipient problems.

Perhaps the biggest error that people make is not to consider their investments a business and to treat them as such. People have jobs, families, personal obligations, and other competing priorities. It's easy to understand how far-away investments get pushed to lower and lower priority, and as long as things are going pretty well they can be ignored.

But in most cases, sooner or later the piper is to be paid, and when things go pear-shaped the losses can quickly accumulate and suddenly what seemed like a good idea has become a major liability. And like most things in life, it takes much more effort to make things right (if they can be made right) than to do them right in the first place.

This may seem like harsh advice, but if you are not prepared to treat your investments as a business and give them the priority they deserve, it might be best to salt your funds away in some safe vehicle that is on auto-pilot and not risk them in the marketplace where circumstances are in constant flux and your input is requisite.

It is easy to see real estate as a passive venture, and it is often presented in that light. Find a decent property at a good price, snap it up, hire a property manager who will get a good tenant, and then sit back while the net rents roll in. In principle, that is how things are supposed to work. But in reality, when the rubber meets the road, that is often – usually – far from how things actually work.

Starting from the initial decision to invest in real estate, to do so through a limited-liability entity such as an LLC or corporation, to pick markets, and select properties, through every other step in the process, there are innumerable points where things can go wrong.

It is said that a real estate investor makes his or her money when buying, not selling, a property, and that is certainly true. Yet it is a commonplace for me to see neophyte investors buying properties with minimal research, often sight-unseen, paying too much up-front, accepting sub-standard renovators and property managers without due diligence and with minimal, if any, guarantees, and allowing small issues to grow into large ones through inadequate attention to their business and properties.

Following the great U.S. real estate crash of 2008-09, numerous investors came from overseas to buy rental properties in this country, often at great values. Some continue to come, and will for some time to come (if they did not, there would be no purpose for this book).

Increasingly, though, I am seeing overseas investors, one after another, become disillusioned with their U.S. investments and to begin to divest themselves of their properties and to shut down their investment vehicles. Many made little or no money on their investments, and some have suffered significant losses.

Based on these experiences, it would be easy to say that U.S. real estate is a risky business and a poor investment. Yet, others have made veritable fortunes in U.S. real estate and earn good income month after month from it. Meanwhile, their properties continue to appreciate and offer further profits down the road.

While some of this might be attributable to that elusive factor known as good luck, in reality and in most cases it is actually attributable to good research, careful planning, letting some "opportunities" go by while jumping on others, and – perhaps more than anything – keeping a close eye on things, running their investments like a business, and limiting their downsides.

Setting realistic objectives is also a key part of the process. It's easy to be led on by promises of 15-20+ percent returns on an investment, and while such returns might be realistic in some cases, one needs to be suspicious. The old adage, that if something seems too good to be true it probably is, certainly applies.

On paper such returns might be possible. But what about emergency repairs? Properties that take twice as long to renovate as was promised? Extended vacancies? Unpredictable misfortunes ranging from tenant theft, absconding property managers, failing major appliances, municipal and homeowner association fines, storm or weather damage, and vandalism? Yes, I have seen *all* of these things happen, and the balance sheet quickly moves from the positive to the negative.

While there are no guarantees to anything in life, there are ways of accounting for and limiting the damage caused by most of these things. But there is one basic principle of investing, and that is that the higher the anticipated returns, the higher the risk. That's why people put money into real estate and other investment vehicles rather than simply keeping their money in the bank. Yet it is unrealistic to expect that high returns will just flow in either without risk or without input and careful planning and ongoing watching by the investor.

What are some of the factors to consider in setting your objectives? Let's list some here:

- Do I want nearly immediate income, or am I willing to wait for a property to be renovated in order to increase the value of my purchase? How long am I willing to wait? How certain am I that the renovator is capable of performing as promised? What guarantees or compensations do I have in place to protect me if the renovator does not perform as expected?

- Am I better off scattering my properties among various markets (and usually various property managers), or to pick one market and concentrate all my holdings in that market?

What is to be gained (or lost) by either approach?

- What is the best way to protect myself and my other holdings and assets from liability that could arise from an unforeseen hazard or simply a litigious party, whether a tenant or a third-party? How much am I willing to put at risk? What are my lines of defense? What is the cost-benefit analysis on this?

- How should I structure my holdings to not only limit my liability but also limit my tax bite? What are the advantages and disadvantages of different kinds of holding and management structures? What are the real tax consequences of investing in different markets and states and through different vehicles? How will local, state, and federal taxes impact on my net income? Have these taxes and other market costs been realistically factored into my analysis?

- How willing am I to stay with a given property manager when problems begin to arise? What due diligence am I willing and able to do on various property managers, or am I just ready to take the manager that is presented to me? How passive or active am I willing to be with my property management?

- How much can I comfortably put at risk, over what time frame, and how much can and should I keep in reserve for either foreseen or unforeseen expenses? How much am I prepared to lose if things go the wrong way, and how quickly can I pull the plug and recover my investment (or what is left of it) if I need to?

- Are there other ways of investing my funds in real estate, such as private-money lending, joint ventures, and property flipping, that offer me security and good returns without all the risk and hassles of holding rental properties?

- Do I want a property that I can use as a vacation home for myself and my family while putting it to work earning income when I'm not using it?

- Do I want to invest directly in real estate or would I be better off investing in a Real Estate Investment Trust (REIT), a kind of security.

(Note that the main focus of this book is on direct investment and does not deal with REITs, shares of which can be bought and sold much like stocks. This is not meant to denigrate REITs or discourage anyone who finds REITs to be their preferred investment type but is simply a limitation imposed on this book's focus.)

There are some important takeaways from this discussion, but the bottom line is that one's basic objectives should be clear and the steps taken to reach them consistent with them.

Most important of all, investors need to stay on top of their investments and treat them like a business. They need to make them a top priority and to give them the time and attention that any business demands. Failure to do so is just asking for problems and losses. And no one who invests their hard-earned funds seeks those.

What State(s)?

Once you've determined your overall investment objectives, you've decided to go ahead with acquiring investment properties in the United States, and you've decided to protect yourself and your assets with an entity structure (and type of entity structure you'll use), the question then becomes which states should you register your entities in?

Aside from registering in states where you hold rental properties, there is a bigger initial issue that needs to be addressed from an asset-protection perspective. And that concerns basing your investment structure in a state with top asset-protection laws and court precedents protective of what is called the "corporate veil."

Three states often are mentioned as being best for asset protection: Delaware, Nevada, and Wyoming. These states are home to numerous corporations and limited liability companies (LLCs) that often do no business in the state but are registered in the state simply due to what is viewed as its highly favorable asset-protection environment.

My own preference, the one I generally recommend to my clients, and the one in which I register my own parent entities, is Wyoming. One can argue the relative advantages of one state over another from morning to night, but Wyoming has much to recommend it.

Like Nevada and Delaware, it has favorable state statutes as well as court rulings protective of the corporate veil, and the sole remedy available to a successful litigant against a Wyoming LLC is what is called a charging order, a key asset-protection element. Wyoming's charging order remedy (described in more detail below) is set by state statute (as also relatively recently was done in Nevada), not merely by judicial decisions.

Additionally, Delaware has served more as a home of large corporations since its jurisprudence largely applies to them, whereas Wyoming is more hospitable to small business entities.

While both Nevada and Wyoming have no state business or personal income taxes, the fees to register and maintain an entity in both Nevada and Delaware are significantly higher than those of Wyoming – the state licensing fee recently even significantly increased by the Nevada legislature – and Delaware does impose a franchise tax on corporations and an equivalent tax that applies to LLCs. These costs make a big difference to the smaller investor, all other things being equal.

Wyoming allows domestication of out-of-state entities, and we're seeing the recent annual cost increases in Nevada serving as an inducement for some Nevada entities to domesticate in Wyoming.

The question arises, what is a charging order? In basic terms, it is a court-authorized right granted to a judgment creditor to attach distributions made from a business entity, such as a LLC or limited partnership, to a debtor who is a member or partner of the business entity. It bars seizure of property owned either by the debtor or the entity.

Wyoming takes this key provision further than some states and applies it to single-member LLCs. This prevents a creditor from foreclosing on a member's interest in even a single-member LLC or interfering in the management of the entity. Somewhat akin to a wage garnishment, the charging order gives a creditor a claim on distributions to a member. It does not, however, require that any distributions be made, so the debtor member could theoretically wait out a creditor claimant. In practice, often the parties will come to some sort of agreement on settling the debt.

Note that the protections offered by the charging order only apply to actions committed by the entity (inside liability) and not to actions committed as individuals (for instance, traffic injuries) by the members or partners of the entities (outside liability). However, by putting real estate holdings in a limited liability entity, this takes them out of the individual's name and can shield them in the case of a lawsuit entailing outside liability.

Further, Wyoming provides excellent privacy protection, allows nominee officers and directors, and is the originator (in 1977) of the initial model U.S.

limited liability company law, since emulated by all other states and numerous countries.

While Nevada often serves as refuge for companies seeking to escape (not always with great success) from neighboring California's onerous taxes, it also tends to attract more attention both from the IRS and the California tax authorities. And the state legislature does, from time-to-time, consider imposing a state tax. Wyoming has so far avoided these downsides and, given its significant mineral wealth, actually has run a budget surplus even through the worst of the downturn that drove many other states to run huge budgetary deficits.

Wyoming's protection of single-member LLCs, along with multi-member LLCs, is superior to that offered by many other states, where courts have allowed a creditor to assume control of and foreclose on single-member LLCs. Wyoming also has a Registered Limited Liability Partnership (RLLP) form – more akin to an LLC than a limited partnership, with protections similar to an LLC – which is the preferred investment vehicle for Canadian investors.

The question arises: If I register an entity in Wyoming, will Wyoming law protect me in other states where I might own properties, either using the Wyoming entity to hold the properties or child entities in which the Wyoming entity is the member? And the definitive answer is: Maybe. There is no set answer to this question since various courts in various states have ruled, and will continue to do so, in various ways on the question, some applying the laws of that state, others deferring to Wyoming law. The same can apply to any entity registered in another state, including Nevada and Delaware.

While any limited liability entity, in any state, is likely to offer better asset protection than operating and holding properties directly as an individual, the Wyoming entity may well offer better protections and enters more favorable elements into the equation. There also are ways (covered in the next chapter on "Structure") of structuring holdings using Wyoming entities that offer further protections as well as potential tax advantages.

It is important that investors treat their LLCs, corporations, and other entities as entities, and not as extensions of themselves or as personal piggy banks or ATMs. This means LLCs – even single-member LLCs – should have well crafted operating agreements, corporations should have bylaws, and partnerships should have partner agreements. Company formalities, such as initial and annual meetings and documenting key decisions through member resolutions, and opening and operating through company business bank accounts (more information on banking in the chapter on "Banking"), are all important elements to establish the "entityhood" and the separate identity of the entity from the investor.

Registering in other states

Once the decision is made to base one's investment structure in a state – like Wyoming, Nevada, or Delaware – with strong asset-protection laws and case history, the next decision concerns registration in the states where the investor acquires properties.

Normally simply owning property in a given state does not require registration to do business in that state because simple property ownership generally is not deemed to be "doing business" in that state. The catch comes in when a state -- as most do -- adds the proviso, "and nothing more," or other such verbiage.

That is where holding properties for rental, which is generally interpreted to mean "something more" under the law, becomes the key factor requiring registration in that state.

A few states, like Minnesota, spell it out specifically -- holding property for rental is considered doing business in the state and requires registration. Some leave the question vague. California, for one, requires registration even for simple property ownership by an LLC or corporation -- and then, in typical California form, adds injury to insult by requiring a minimum $800 annual tax, whether or not the entity takes in even a penny. In any case, most states cover the issue with the "and nothing more" proviso in their company registration law.

To help address the question, I personally contacted the offices of the secretaries of state in more than a dozen states, including just about all the states where our clients own rental properties as well as several others, and got back virtually the same answer from all of them: They only process documents and cannot give legal advice. An attorney should be contacted for further guidance, but it is the entity's responsibility to determine if they are within the requirements of the law.

Of course, it is usually less expensive and easier just to register in the state and not pay legal fees to find out that you need to register anyway.

There are other good reasons why investors should register their companies in states where the companies hold rental properties, even in those rare cases where there is an element of doubt. Without registering, the company can always be sued. But if for some reason the company needs to file a law suit, it is normally barred from doing so for lack of standing in the state if it is not registered to do business in that state.

So, if the occasion arises to sue a tenant for non-payment, or to institute an eviction, or to sue a property manager for non-performance, or any other reason, your company will be barred from filing that law suit until it is duly registered in the state.

There also can be other serious, and in some cases costly, downsides for failing to register in a state where you hold rental properties and are required to register. For one, most states have penalties -- in some cases, such as in the case of

Texas, severe penalties -- for failing to register when registration is required. In almost all cases this includes registering, payment of all back annual or other fees, and often additional penalties. A state can cross-reference against tax filings and determine if a company failed to register. And there are other downsides, such as the one mentioned where filing lawsuits would be barred, and these can apply even when registration is not clearly required. Some states, like Georgia, also apply back-up withholding of state taxes upon sale of properties if the owning entity failed to register in the state. So, the easy answer is, it is best to register in any state where you hold rental properties and avoid serious problems down the road.

There are different approaches to how a company might register in any given state. In some states, the fees are the same whether you are registering a domestic (in-state) entity or a foreign (out-of-state) one. In other states, it is considerably more costly to register a foreign entity for what is usually called a Certificate of Authority to operate in that state, versus registering a new domestic entity in it. And some states differentiate between the fees for corporations and LLCs, and it can work both ways: Some states charge more on an initial and ongoing basis for corporations, others charge more for LLCs. Don't assume there is any logic, reason, or predictability to these variables.

I would suggest looking beyond merely the initial and ongoing costs of registration (as important as these can be) to determine how to approach registration in any given state. How good are the state's asset-protection laws and environment? What is your risk profile, and how do you want to divide up your holdings in line with it? Have you already signed a buy-sell agreement, or even already closed, on a given property in one of your entity's names? What does your investment structure look like? Are there any external restrictions (such as the legal proscription against an entity held by an Australian Self-Managed Superannuation Fund owning any other entities) that would prohibit registration of child entities below a parent entity?

Even in cases where registration fees for a foreign entity are higher, you might still come out ahead financially – if your risk profile and other factors permit it – to register a parent company to do business in another state since you're avoiding the costs of a separate operating agreement, potential superfluous accounting and consulting fees, and other ongoing costs of maintaining multiple companies.

But in states with relatively good asset-protection laws, as well as high foreign-entity registration fees – Texas, again, comes to mind – it might be advisable to register a new domestic entity in the state. See also the discussion in the chapter on "Structure" of how a court might treat a foreign entity registered in a state versus a domestic child entity of a member entity registered in a state, like Wyoming, with top asset-protection laws.

Note that, by default, the IRS considers single-member LLCs to be disregarded pass-through entities for tax purposes. In other words, by default a single-member LLC does not file its own federal tax return or pay its own federal taxes. These are passed through to the ultimate member, who files and pays the federal taxes at whatever rate applies to the member. An LLC with two or more members is considered a partnership by the IRS, with taxes apportioned between, and then passed through to, the members.

I stress *federal* taxes since some states might require a single-member LLC to file its own state return, though in general state returns are based to varying degrees on the ultimate federal return filed. And even if your filing entity is registered in a state without a state tax, you will still owe taxes to those states with state taxes where you generate revenues.

An LLC can file an election with the IRS to be taxed as an entity, like a corporation or association, at corporate tax rates, but it must make the election to be so treated. As you can see, U.S. taxation is a bit of a morass at both the federal and state levels and requires careful treading to avoid the many landmines attached to it. The later chapter of this book on "Tax Matters" looks at various tax issues.

It helps to look ahead and map out on paper how you plan to set up your investment structure. This would include any parent or head structure as well as the individual state registrations of child entities or foreign registrations. It also is helpful to set up a calendar and tickler system for tending to various state responsibilities such as filing annual reports and paying annual fees, as well as filing state tax returns.

Finally, it may be that you already own rental properties through an entity in a state or states where you have failed to register the entity. In those cases, the only practical route -- short of doing title changes and taking other time-consuming and potentially costly steps -- is registering the owning entity for a Certificate of Authority to operate in those states. As noted, in some (not all) cases the filing fees will be higher, but normally this is the least costly and troublesome route to take.

In practical terms, you can attempt to go under the radar and declare that you are just beginning to do business in the state, and from experience we can say that this tactic usually works and – while no guarantees are offered – most states don't challenge this contention for the small investor. But it is important not to delay until a state makes the determination that you are not in compliance with its laws and does attempt to levy penalties, or you need to file a lawsuit.

Before departing this section, I want to make mention of what are called Series LLCs. Currently 15 states, the District of Columbia, and Puerto Rico allow for this form of LLC. It is held out as a way that multiple properties can be held in separate LLCs without the ongoing expense of separate LLCs, but there are both advantages and disadvantages to the Series LLC form. See a discussion of Series LLCs in the FAQs section of this book.

I hope this clarifies the important issues concerning entity registrations in the various states and helps keep you from running afoul of the law. While this cannot be considered formal legal advice, this guidance is based on our experience and best understanding in this area. Ultimately, the decision whether to register in a given state or not is your responsibility.

Structure

How you structure your holdings is a basic element that should be part of your planning. It is important to your asset protection, but it also helps avoid needless trouble and expense and allows you to be more efficient in setting up your investment structure.

There are some essential things to consider in planning your structure:

- How will you hold your U.S. investment structure. As an individual? Through a domestic company in your home country? Through a partnership? Through a family trust? Through a special retirement vehicle?

- How do you want your income to be taxed? This will be a factor in whether you operate through, or are taxed as, a corporation or as a limited liability company (LLC), which is by default a pass-through entity for tax purposes.

- How many, and what types, of properties do you plan to acquire? And in what and how many states?

- How much liability are you prepared to assume?

- Would a split ownership / management / finance structure benefit you?

I want to go back to something I said in the Introduction to this book: It is not how much you make on your investments, as how much you keep, that matters. That is why I recommend that you plan a structure as simple and cost-effective as possible to accomplish your objectives and provide you with the protection you need.

If you are just planning on holding one or a few single-family homes in one state, your structure is likely to be much different than if you are planning on holding a number of properties in several states, or if your holdings will include apartments or commercial properties. We'll look at the different levels of asset-protection structure complexity and from them you can design the one that works best for you.

It would be useful for you to read the chapter on "What State(s)?" if you have not already done so to make better sense of this chapter. We will look at three different basic structures – which we'll call "Good," "Better," and "Best" asset protection – in order from simplest to most complex. But keep in mind that there might be variations on these that better suit your particular circumstances or objectives.

"Good" Asset Protection: The Simplest Structure

For the smaller investor, this structure provides basic asset protection and helps keep costs and complexity to a minimum. Refer to the "Good Asset Protection" chart for illustration. Holding your investment properties through an entity, most likely a limited liability company, and treating that entity as an entity separate from yourself, is the most basic and perhaps most important step you can take to protect your personal assets.

"Good" Asset Protection Chart

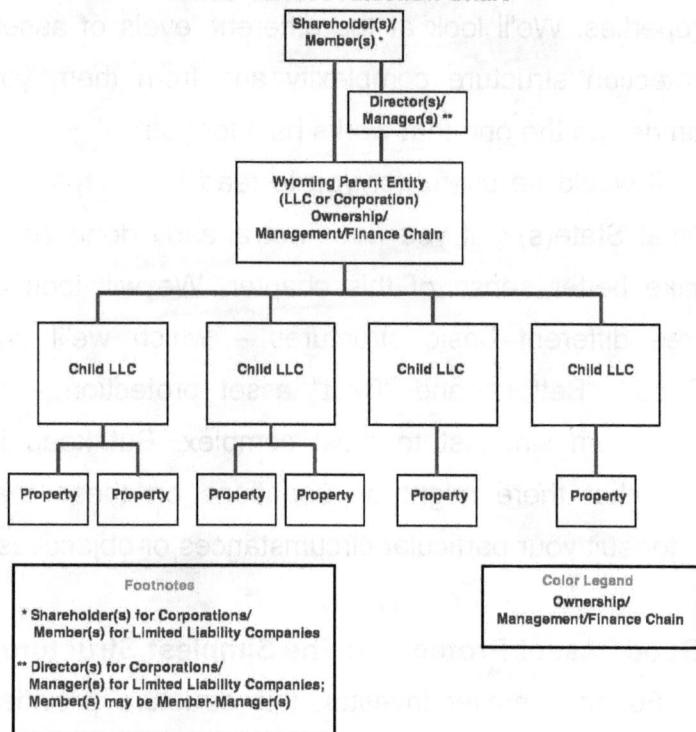

```
        ┌─────────────────────┐
        │   Shareholder(s)/   │
        │     Member(s) *     │
        └──────────┬──────────┘
                   │
        ┌──────────┴──────────┐
        │    Director(s)/     │
        │    Manager(s) **    │
        └──────────┬──────────┘
                   │
    ┌──────────────┴──────────────┐
    │   Wyoming Parent Entity      │
    │   (LLC or Corporation)       │
    │   Ownership/                 │
    │   Management/Finance Chain   │
    └──────────────┬──────────────┘
```

Child LLC	Child LLC	Child LLC	Child LLC

Property	Property	Property	Property	Property	Property

Footnotes

* Shareholder(s) for Corporations/
   Member(s) for Limited Liability Companies

** Director(s) for Corporations/
    Manager(s) for Limited Liability Companies;
    Member(s) may be Member-Manager(s)

Color Legend
Ownership/
Management/Finance Chain

The first step, in my view of how this structure should be set up, is to register an entity in Wyoming. This will be the parent or anchor entity, and it can be a corporation or an LLC, depending on your tax and other considerations (see other parts of this guide for more information on the pluses and minuses of different kinds of entities). I won't go into all the benefits of establishing your structure in Wyoming here, nor pretend that this by itself is a panacea – see the chapter on "What State(s)?" But to my way of thinking, this offers your best choice for asset protection and that, after all, is the purpose of owning your properties through an entity.

As noted in the chapter on "What State(s)?," you'll then have to register in whatever state or states where you hold your properties. This can be done either by registering new domestic (in this context, this means in-state) child entities (most likely LLCs) in those states with the Wyoming parent as Member-Manager of them, or registering the Wyoming parent as a foreign (out-of-state) entity in those states for what is generally called a Certificate of Authority to do business in those states.

In some states, as previously noted, it can be considerably more to register a foreign, versus domestic, entity, so the latter option might be the most cost-effective one to follow in those cases.

According to this model (as in all three models), a property-holding LLC (which may be a child of a parent entity or a direct registration of a primary entity) may hold anywhere from one to several properties, again depending on the risk profile the investor wishes or is prepared to take on.

In the case of parent-child entity relationships, according to this model normally the parent entity is Member-Manager of a child LLC.

Note that if you register your Wyoming entity as a foreign entity in another state, you are agreeing to make it subject to the laws and judicial precedents of that state. If you register a child entity in another state, in the event of a law suit it is more likely that the courts will refer back to the member, which is a Wyoming entity subject to Wyoming law. Consequently, registering a child entity with your Wyoming entity as parent may well (though not definitely) offer you more protection than registering your Wyoming entity as a foreign entity.

While there are potentially more costs of setting up a child entity, such as having an operating agreement and initial meeting minutes prepared, this might still be an advantageous route to take and, in some states, would help balance out the additional costs of registering a foreign entity.

Note that some investment vehicles, such as Australian Self-Managed Superannuation Funds

(SMSFs), do not allow fund-owned entities to own other entities, so the only two options for investors working through those kinds of funds is to either register their Wyoming parent entity or entities as foreign entities in the states where the properties are located, or to register a fund-owned primary entity directly in those states, foregoing the benefits of a Wyoming registration.

"Better" Asset Protection: A Bifurcated Structure

Many, perhaps most, actionable torts arise out of the management function. This alone provides a key reason to separate the management function from the ownership structure of your investments. In doing so, it is important that any management entity established does not own any meaningful assets of its own so that, in the event of a successful lawsuit against it, there is nothing for a litigant to gain. The things that can lead to litigation and which are related to management include such things as code violations, defective structural elements, breakdown of key systems such as heat, water, or sanitation systems, utility turn-offs due to delayed or missed utility payments, and any number of other things.

"Better" Asset Protection Chart

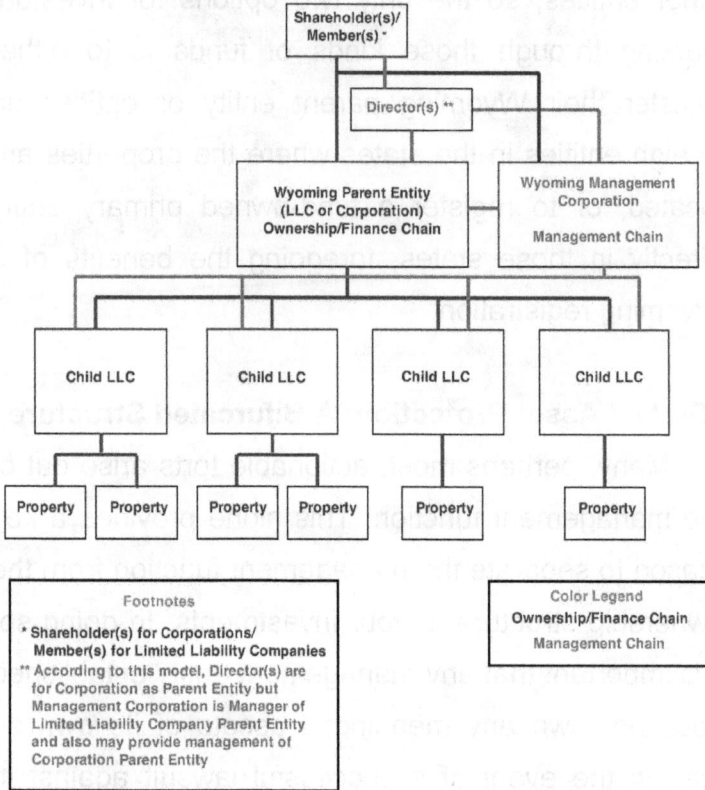

```
                    Shareholder(s)/
                    Member(s) *
                          |
                    Director(s) **
                    /            \
   Wyoming Parent Entity      Wyoming Management
   (LLC or Corporation)           Corporation
   Ownership/Finance Chain
                                Management Chain

   Child LLC   Child LLC   Child LLC   Child LLC

Property Property  Property Property  Property  Property
```

Footnotes

* Shareholder(s) for Corporations/
  Member(s) for Limited Liability Companies
** According to this model, Director(s) are
  for Corporation as Parent Entity but
  Management Corporation is Manager of
  Limited Liability Company Parent Entity
  and also may provide management of
  Corporation Parent Entity

Color Legend
Ownership/Finance Chain
Management Chain

While you are likely to turn over day-to-day property management functions to a professional property management company, the property manager works for you so any liability would extend to both the property manager and to you.

If you separate your management function as the source of any litigation from your asset-owning entity to your management entity you are lowering the liability profile of your asset-owning entity. This is a key reason why many LLCs will employ outside managers rather than being member-managed.

There also is a potential tax benefit to separating your management function from your ownership function, using a Wyoming-based management entity. Wyoming has no state business or personal income taxes, which most other states – including states where you might hold properties – do. By charging a reasonable (key word!) management fee to your other entities, you may be able to move a portion of your income from a tax state to non-tax Wyoming. While this is a wash for federal taxation, since expenditures and income balance out, it might help lower your state-level tax bite.

Normally a management entity will be structured as a corporation rather than an LLC. The corporation can deduct all expenses from taxable income, reducing its federal tax burden. Additionally, a corporation can offer some benefits, such as a corporate health benefits plan, that an LLC cannot, but these are ancillary to the main purpose of a management corporation, which is asset protection. Since it is not a pass-through entity, the corporation does not add to the ultimate beneficiary's tax burden unless it pays out shareholder dividends, which it is under no obligation to do.

The "Better Asset Protection" chart illustrates this approach to asset protection.

An LLC, which by default is considered managed by its member or members, makes itself manager-managed through a provision in its company operating agreement. It is also useful to include a member resolution to this effect, and to put in place a management agreement between the LLC (or a corporation that wishes to employ a management entity) and the management entity, spelling out specific terms, such as fees and duties.

"Best" Asset Protection: A Three-Pronged Structure for Maximum Protection

While the "Good" approach insulates the beneficiaries' assets from seizure and the "Better" approach removes most potentially tortious actions from the ownership chain, the "Best" approach to asset protection also effectively removes asset value from the properties owned by the limited liability entities. Thus, even if a litigant is successful, there is little or no value to be gained through a successful law suit. In fact, this might discourage potential litigants from even filing suit in the first place. This approach works best where the investor is supplying some or all of the funds for acquiring properties himself or herself, as is often the reality. In cases where third-party lenders are supplying a portion of the funds to acquire properties, there will be mortgages on the properties that remove much of the asset value from the properties.

Whether the investor is supplying all the funds or just a portion of them, doing so through a dedicated finance entity takes the asset value out of the ownership chain and moves it to the separate finance entity. The LLC owning the property gives a mortgage or deed of trust, as mortgages are called in some states, to the finance entity in return for the property funding, and so has greatly reduced its asset value. The only asset value it holds is any non-mortgaged equity that might exist in a given property. This normally will be a relatively small percentage of the overall property value.

Note that any loans made to the owning entity should not be made as a general loan but rather made through mortgages on the owned properties to strip equity value out of the properties.

"Best" Asset Protection Chart

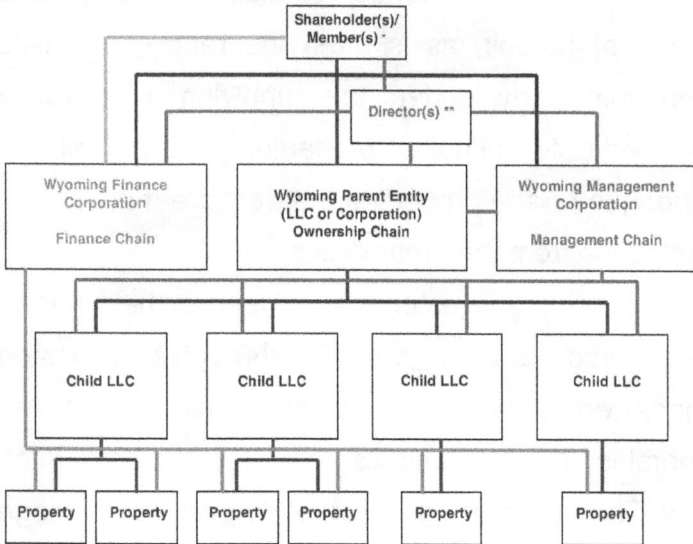

Shareholder(s)/ Member(s) *

Director(s) **

Wyoming Finance Corporation

Finance Chain

Wyoming Parent Entity (LLC or Corporation) Ownership Chain

Wyoming Management Corporation

Management Chain

Child LLC

Child LLC

Child LLC

Child LLC

Property Property Property Property Property Property

Footnotes

* Shareholder(s) for Corporations/ Member(s) for Limited Liability Companies

** According to this model, Director(s) are for Corporations as Parent, Finance, and Management entities, but Management Corporation is Manager of Limited Liability Company Parent Entity and also may provide management of Corporation Parent Entity

Color Legend

Ownership Chain
Management Chain
Finance Chain

In this approach to asset protection, illustrated by the "Best Asset Protection" chart, the ownership, management, and finance functions are all separate from one another, and all run (ideally) through Wyoming entities with their superior asset protections. In this approach, along with setting up a separate Wyoming management corporation, the investor also sets up a separate Wyoming finance corporation. The investor funds the finance corporation which in turn provides the finance to acquire properties to the holding entities and, in return, takes back mortgages on the financed properties.

While removing equity from the ownership chain, thus providing asset protection benefits, there also are tax benefits to be realized from state-level taxes. The interest paid on the mortgages serves as a deduction from state taxes and is paid to the Wyoming entity, with no state tax levies on the income. Again, the effect on federal taxes is neutral, but this approach can move some income from tax states to non-tax Wyoming.

A few points need to be noted about this approach. First, not all finance sources (such as Australian SMSFs) may allow funding through a finance entity. Also, this is the most costly structure to set up and to maintain, with both annual corporate costs and potential consultant costs. It is, therefore, recommended more in cases where an investor's holdings justify the added expense, and it may not be suitable for all holdings.

The Registration Process

The first thing to know about the entity registration process is that it varies, often considerably, by state, can be different for LLCs versus corporations, and often is different for in-state (domestic) entities versus out-of-state (foreign) ones. In reality, there is no set registration process when you get down to the details, though the steps are generally similar, if not identical, between the various states.

We'll cover the general process here, but it's simply not practical to detail every state's processes and requirements. Even as someone who does this all the time, for a living, in numerous states, it is not uncommon for some new wrinkle to present itself to me in dealing with a specific situation.

Once you've set out your objectives, decided on your structure, and have determined what state or states you are going to register in, the steps are similar in both order and process.

Name check

Every entity needs a name. But many names are already in use, and some are even trademarked. And a name that is available or acceptable in one state may be neither in another.

A general rule is that the more unusual the name you select, the better your chances of it being available. Also, most states allow add-ons, such as adding the word "property" or "investment" or "holdings" to a root name, to render a name unique and therefore able to be registered. Most states allow geographic designators to make a name unique, such as "Georgia," "St. Louis," or "North America," but one exception to this is Texas, which does not.

Reading the naming rules, often available on a given state's Secretary of State site, can help, but the rules can be confusing or unclear, too. One especially tricky thing is when a name that reads differently on paper but sounds the same as another one when spoken is disallowed. An example: "Jacks Car Service" versus "Jax Car Service."

Some names are disallowed on their face. Besides names that might be considered obscene or blasphemous, names that include what are normally licensed activities – like those containing words like "bank," "insurance," or "fund" – would be disallowed absent a license to operate in the field to which the name applies.

Also, an entity normally needs to indicate in its name that it is an entity, and the type. For instance, a limited liability company normally must include the words "Limited Liability Company" or the abbreviations "L.L.C." or "LLC" in its name. A corporation normally needs to include "Corporation," "Corp.," "Incorporated," or "Inc." in its name, or whatever other terms a given state permits. A registered limited liability partnership would include those words or the abbreviations "R.L.L.P." or "RLLP" in its name.

The entity designator does not make a name unique (i.e., "Holiday Holdings LLC" would not be allowed if there is a "Holiday Holdings Inc."), and neither does punctuation, including whether there is a comma after the main name and the designator (i.e., "Holiday Holdings, LLC" versus "Holiday Holdings LLC"), or spelling out "and" versus using an ampersand ("&").

If your entity already has a name in one state that is not available in a state in which it intends to register (either because it is being used as a company name or held as a trade name), two choices present themselves. The entity can choose to operate under a different, available, name in the other state, or it has to obtain written permission from the holder of the name in the other state to use the name. This includes other entities that also belong to you. The state will not register the company until either route is selected and whatever evidence of permission (and normally a fee) that is required is presented with the registration. So a good thing to do is to check out a name in all states in which you envisage possibly operating to be sure there are no conflicts.

We always ask for at least three distinct choices of names, in preference order, so that the chances of running into a conflict is greatly reduced. Even then, it sometimes happens there is a conflict. Until the state registers a name, there are no guarantees.

Most states allow free name checks, so the chances of finding an available name is greatly increased before starting the registration process. Texas, again, is an exception to this rule in that name checks carry a fee that is only waived when the name check leads to registration of a company as part of the process.

States also allow a name that is allowable to be put on hold for a certain time, with the payment of a fee. I don't find this particularly useful unless you are not going to be registering the company for some time and are really set on a given name for it. Names also can pertain to dead or dissolved companies or trade name registrations, and each state varies as to when such names may again be used. Often a call to the Secretary of State's office can help obtain clarity on naming issues at no cost.

One other rule of thumb to keep in mind when selecting a name for an entity is that it is generally not a good idea to use your own name or your family name as all or part of the name of the entity. The whole idea of an entity is to separate it and its liability profile from your own personal identity.

While giving the entity your name does not automatically mean that you are using it for personal purposes, it can be used as one more piece of evidence by a litigant to say that the entity is really just an alter-ego for you and so the so-called "corporate veil" should be pierced. It also gives away your identity, which you may wish to preserve to make it more difficult for a litigant to reach you. Last but not least, naming a corporation after yourself may lead the IRS to conclude that it is what is called a "Personal Service Corporation" and therefore subject to much higher taxation rates. Again, this is not a given, but why tempt fate or the powers that be by using your own or your family name as the entity name?

Completing the Articles

Limited liability companies are created through filing what usually are called Articles of Organization or Articles of Formation. A corporation is created through filing Articles of Incorporation (often called Articles or Memorandum of Association in Britain and other countries whose corporate law is based on

British law, terms not generally known or used in the U.S.)

These Articles are filed with the Secretary of State or, in a few states, special corporate divisions separate from the SecState, and upon acceptance the state often issues a Certificate of Organization (or Formation) or Certificate of Incorporation to the entity.

Many states allow uniquely drafted Articles of Incorporation to be filed, and these might contain provisions, allowed by law in that state, that pertain specifically to that corporation. LLCs, on the other hand, normally will craft any special provisions into an operating agreement. We'll cover these documents elsewhere in this book.

Again, I have to resort to use of words like "often," "generally," "sometimes," "most," and other non-definitive qualifiers since so many variations exist between states, and often within states, depending on the situation.

Most states have set forms – either paper forms, online forms, or both – to use when filing Articles. Some states allow online filing in some cases, others work entirely with paper processes, and some have both. Some states require setting up a user account to do online filings, while others don't. Some states are fairly loose when it comes to how information can be entered on a given form, while others have very strict and often arcane and unwritten rules for this (Pennsylvania comes to mind). Some states, such as Ohio, permit faxed or scanned signatures, while others (like Wyoming) require everything to be original. And a few go both ways, depending on what it is that is being faxed or scanned. One state that I know of – North Dakota – even allows entirely faxed filings, with payment of fees by credit card.

The same panoply of variations exists for filing annual reports and paying annual fees, which some, but not all, states require, though usually these may be filed online.

Filing fees also vary all over the map (literally!), as does how any given state provides evidence of registration. Some will send back stamped hard copies of the registration papers, others will only provide electronic versions (without paying additionally for paper copies), and some only provide "evidence" of having received and filed the registration.

You may be wondering if you can file your own company registrations or if you need to work with a filing service or even an attorney. As I said at the outset to this book, you should consult an attorney for any legal issues you may have, and an accountant for any financial or tax issues on which you have questions. But, in my view, it is overkill – and usually vastly more expensive – to have an attorney file most company registrations.

With some research and a bit of trial-and-error, you can do company filings on your own, but using a document filing service, whether it is the service I provide or another, often is money well spent, owing in no small part to all the variations and idiosyncrasies noted here. The relatively small cost of a document filing service, well below what most attorneys charge (assuming they are not attorneys masquerading as document filing services, or vice versa), will remove much of the worry and hassle from the process and keep you from making some basic mistakes.

The registered agent

All states require all entities to maintain either a registered agent (called a statutory agent in some states) or a registered office in the state. The sole purpose of the registered agent or, where permitted, office, is to allow for service of legal papers on the company. Clients often ask why they need a registered agent, and this is the reason.

The name and address of the registered agent, or the address of the company's registered office, need to be included in the initial company filing. Failure to maintain a registered agent or office usually will result in the state administratively dissolving the entity.

Some states allow company principals or officers to serve as agents for their companies, but a street address – often a commercial address or actual office – is required in those states. If you don't live in a state or have an office in it, your alternative is to use a registered agent. And not to unduly complicate matters, but a few states not only require you to have a registered agent, but also to have an actual "place of business" (really, in practice, any address you can use normally will do) in the state.

The registered agent address may or may not be shown as the "Principal Office" on the company registration. But this is a formality only and listing that address, when allowed, does not convey any special privileges on the company. Specifically, it may not use the registered agent address for its mail, absent payment of what usually is a significant fee when that agent does agree to handle client mail.

Again, a document filing service often will have arrangements with companies that provide registered agent service, and using such a service saves you the task of identifying and signing up with an agent.

What next?

Performing a name check, selecting a registered agent, and registering a company with the state are just the first steps in setting up a company. Some states (such as Nevada) require you to file a list of company principals and also to obtain a business license, both of which carry significant fees and must be repeated annually.

Many states require you to register with state tax authorities (Pennsylvania, for one, includes this as part of the registration process). Some (like New York and, again, Pennsylvania for corporations) require legal notices to be placed announcing the company's registration. Some require registration with the state's labor bureau. And one state – California – "imputes" a minimum tax to an LLC or corporation, and will charge it a minimum annual state tax of $800 even if the entity does not earn a penny of income in the state, and the "normal" tax rates the state imposes still apply.

Beyond state requirements and peculiarities, there are some general things that all companies, regardless of state of registration, need to accomplish as part of their set-up process. The most important is putting in place a company operating agreement for an LLC, or bylaws for a corporation.

While most states don't require these documents, they are very important – even for single-member LLCs and single-shareholder corporations – to establish as part of the company's asset-protection program. They also help with company governance and answer questions that might arise in the course of running, expanding, transferring, or dissolving the company, or in the event of a governing party's death or incapacitation.

Another important step is applying for an Employer Identification Number (EIN) for the new company. Just as individuals have tax identifying numbers (Social Security Numbers, or SSNs, for U.S.

citizens and legal residents, Individual Tax Identification Numbers, or ITINs, for non-U.S. individuals), a company needs an EIN. For those already holding a U.S. tax number (an SSN or an EIN for an entity higher on the chain of ownership for instance), EINs usually can be applied for online. But for non-U.S. parties who lack a U.S. tax number, the current process requires that the initial application be faxed to the IRS.

Along with the company registration, the EIN will be necessary to open a bank account for the new company. An LLC also needs to decide if it will be considered a disregarded (pass-through) entity (single-member LLC) or partnership (multi-member LLC) for tax purposes, as it is by default, or if it will file an election to be taxed as an association or corporation for tax purposes.

While a corporation can opt to be an "S" corporation for tax purposes (with income passed through to the shareholders, much like an LLC), non-U.S. parties are not allowed to be shareholders in an "S" corporation, so the default tax status of a "C" corporation is the only option for corporations, or

57

LLCs that elect to be treated as corporations for tax purposes, with non-U.S. principals or shareholders.

Banking and tax considerations are covered in more detail in the chapters pertaining to those topics.

Banking

Business and investing is about money. And that means your business needs banking. Seems simple enough, doesn't it?

Unfortunately, it has become virtually impossible for a non-U.S. citizen or resident to open a U.S. bank account without making a personal appearance. And in some cases, even making a personal appearance to open one account does not guarantee that the same bank will open another account for the same party without another personal appearance. You're looking for logic here? Don't.

The banks blame their personal appearance policies on the USA Freedom Act, the new name of the law dealing with security issues that Congress passed, initially as the U.S. Patriot Act, in the wake of the 9-11 attacks of 2001. The law says that banks should know their customers, and the way most banks have interpreted this is to require a personal appearance. Unfortunately, this imposes a great inconvenience on non-U.S. investors, and it can even make it impossible for them to open bank accounts for their companies.

At a time when the U.S. economy would benefit from foreign investment, the banks make it as hard as possible for the foreign investor. And they pass the blame to Congress. The intent is to keep terrorist organizations from raising and transmitting funds via the U.S. banking system, but unfortunately it makes it difficult for legitimate investors to function.

All right. That's the reality, and my gripe about it. Now let's take a look at how you should set up your banking, starting with what you'll need to produce to open a business bank account.

The first thing you'll need will be the Articles of Organization (or Formation) or Articles of Incorporation for your company. You'll need an Employer Identification Number (EIN) for the entity. You might need a banking resolution or some kind of documentation giving you authority to open an account and sign on behalf of the company. You'll also need your personal identification, in the form of a passport and possibly your driver license. And you'll need or at least find useful a U.S. mailing address (preferably not at a major mailing center which might show up in the bank's computer system and which the bank will refuse to accept).

Some banks might ask for additional documentation or verification of funds. If you are missing some of the required documentation the banker normally can accept what you have and hold opening the account in abeyance subject to you supplying the missing items.

Don't be too surprised if a banker doesn't know what Articles look like from various states, or even their own state (yes, I actually have had this happen). They also might say something like you have to be a company manager to be able to open the account (not true – all you need is authority, which you issue yourself, to open and sign for the account) or that they don't open accounts for overseas clients (rarely the case).

My advice is that if the banker starts to say such things or otherwise show ignorance of the basics, thank them for their time and go elsewhere to open your account. You are very likely at the beginning of a long road with many bumps and potholes in it. And whatever else you do, don't back yourself into a corner where you only have one banking option open to you and you are late getting to the airport.

Okay, let's assume you've been able to make a personal appearance at a U.S. bank, found a U.S. bank that will let you open an account without a personal appearance, or found a bank overseas that will enable you to hold U.S. dollar accounts and be able to make and receive fund transfers to and from the U.S., as some will. You've made your way through the maze of requirements to open an account, and you're ready to do so. How should you structure your business banking?

Let's start with the really bad ideas, and then go from there. Some people think they can set up a personal bank account and then run their business finances out of that account. While I would suggest that you also have a personal bank account for your own personal activities in the U.S., a personal bank account should never be used as your business bank account.

From an asset-protection perspective, you need to treat your entity as separate from yourself. As previously noted in other chapters, you can't use it as your personal piggy bank or ATM and then expect that a creditor or even the IRS will not attempt to show that your business is just an extension of yourself.

Another idea that I've seen promoted, and which I advise against, is to have just one bank account for all your entities, perhaps in the name of the parent entity or in that of whatever child entity is most active. As I have consistently said, this is a bad idea, from at least two perspectives.

From the asset-protection perspective, if a creditor or litigant comes after you and is able to get a court order permitting them to seize your bank accounts, if you have all your money from all your entities – including those not subject to the claim of the creditor or litigant – in one account, guess what? They have just seized all your funds, and you're now effectively out of business. How do I know this? I hate to admit it, but I learned this lesson from hard experience.

There is a more mundane reason to have a separate account for each entity, even those that are in a parent-child relationship. Increasingly banks will not accept what are called third-party checks. So let's say your property manager writes you a check for XYZ LLC, but your bank account is in the name of ABC LLC. Previously, you could endorse the check in the name of XYZ LLC and then make it payable for deposit to the account of ABC LLC. But more and more banks are refusing to accept such checks and are returning them.

What do you do then when you're overseas and cannot receive funds owed you because you don't have a bank account in the payee company's name? Yes, we've seen this happen – even regularly now – with clients, and it's not a pretty picture.

So let me make this real simple for you: Open a separate business bank account for each and every entity that you hold. Should I repeat that? Open a separate bank account for each and every entity that you hold. Got it?

Yes, you'll have to pay more fees and incur more expenses (and collect a lot more paper or electronic statements) if you have a bunch of companies, but those are small prices to pay for the clear advantages of doing things this way. On the plus side, usually you can link your various accounts on your online banking, which makes it easy to manage the accounts and transfer funds, as necessary, between them.

There are some other general principles to apply when dealing with American banks. For one, if you have a choice between a good (key word) regional bank and one of the megabanks, you're probably going to get better service and more consideration from the regional bank than the megabank. Almost all banks now offer online banking, so it is no longer a justification to go with the megabank when you can find a good regional bank that offers the same online features. And possibly at less cost.

With interstate banking, it is not essential to open your account in the same state where your companies or properties are located. In fact, it might be a good idea to keep your accounts in a bank far away from where you operate to make it harder to locate your banking and funds should you become embroiled in litigation. Besides, all the megabanks and many regional banks cross state lines with their branches and reach.

Take a good look at the fees that banks charge for different actions as well as any ongoing service fees. These can vary significantly, and you want to try to find a bank that offers you the least cost for those things you need to do most often.

Most banks will give you a debit card that you can use to make charges against your account balance. And most offer a Bill Pay system (which might go under a different name) to enable you to pay bills and move funds around without having to write checks yourself or resort to costly wire transfers. Recurring payments also can be set up. For some payees Bill Pay can do electronic payments, while for others a check will be cut and mailed to the payee. This may be different from what you are used to with banks in your home country.

One can go into detail about various security devices and procedures that different banks employ, such as security cards or keys, to initiate wire transfers or withdrawals, but each bank has a different approach, so suffice it to say that one must deal with whatever procedure or device a given bank employs.

I've seen a number of clients who thought they could get by without checks to go with their business bank accounts. Maybe you are able to function in a check-free world in your home country or for personal business, but for some things you are going to need checks, or at least find them highly functional, in the U.S. For instance, a client recently asked us to write a check for a water utility deposit and turn-on fee when the utility would not accept a credit card payment for this purpose, and a wire transfer would have cost far more. Some places also require that property taxes be paid by check or draft.

You should get a small set of starter checks when you open a new business checking account – ask for them if the banker doesn't offer them – and these may suffice for awhile. But if you need to write more than the small number of checks in the starter book you'll need to order a box of regular checks for your accounts. The cost is not great in the scale of things, but the utility often is.

And one more key point: Get to know at least one person at the branch where you open your accounts, probably the banker whose desk you sit at to set up the accounts. Pick up one – make it two or three, even better – of the banker's cards, and put them in your check book and anywhere else you'll know where to find them. When problems arise, this person becomes your personal contact with the bank and is usually the first person to call on to resolve a problem or answer a question. And don't be surprised if that person suddenly disappears one day. Quickly find a replacement person – a specific individual – to serve as your personal banker, and get their contact information, including their direct phone number and email address.

Note that at the time of this writing interest rates paid by U.S. banks are almost non-existent. With business bank accounts, often the best you can hope for is an account with low monthly fees or, in some cases, no monthly fees at all. In the case of interest-bearing accounts, such as personal or business savings accounts, the bank will have you complete and sign a Form W-8BEN, W-8BEN-E, or W-8ECI, depending on your circumstances, for yourself or on behalf of your entity to determine if you are subject to what is called back-up withholding of tax. It is important to complete these, and don't be surprised if the bank gives you some arcane reason why they need you to do them over.

Note that unless you are a U.S. citizen or legal resident, you should not complete a Form W-9, which overseas investors often are erroneously asked to complete. Instead, you should be asked to complete one of the W-8 forms.

And you thought this was going to be simple!

Finance

Finance allows investors to leverage – that is, extend – their own funds, so this is a key element of most investment strategies. It also has proven to be one of the thorniest issues for the non-U.S. investor to deal with in the U.S.

That said, there are avenues open to the non-U.S. investor for obtaining finance that, while sometimes fraught with limitations and caveats, can be obtained by some investors. Additionally, there are alternatives to acquiring properties that enable non-U.S. investors to actually become lenders themselves. More on this interesting approach later in this chapter.

One of the problems in discussing finance, which almost led me to leave out this chapter altogether, is that there are few hard and fast rules. Circumstances change, lender policies come and go, and much depends on the individual investor's situation and what a given lender will consider or require.

There also is more than one way to skin the proverbial cat, and we'll take a look at some of those, too. Let's dig in, starting with some finance basics and going from there.

Finance basics

The credit reporting system in the U.S. is similar to that used in some countries and drastically different from that of many other countries. Credit reports from your home country will most likely be inapplicable in the U.S., just as U.S. credit reports aren't usable in your country.

Some countries, like Canada, the U.K., Germany, Singapore, South Africa, and some others, have credit reporting systems similar to that in the U.S., and in some countries reports are even put together by the same companies. Others, like Australia, can

71

have markedly different systems, and this can lead to frustrations.

Lenders in many countries depend on looking at an individual's finances and repayment history on a case-by-case basis for their decisions. Having been through this process while living overseas in other countries, it bears some similarity to what is done in the U.S., absent the credit report and overriding credit scores.

What is generally not known, even by Americans, is that the so-called FICO® score (named after the Fair Isaac Corporation that developed it going back to the 1950s) is actually used today ". . . in more than 20 countries on five continents as well as by the top 50 U.S. financial institutions, the 25 largest U.S. credit card issuers and the 25 largest U.S. auto lenders."[1]

Yet in practice, U.S. lenders often do look at a number of different factors including the individual's overall credit record, income, assets, and scores issued by the three major credit reporting agencies, which can differ both between each other and with the FICO® score, though how they are derived is similar. Also, the standards for one type of loan is likely different from those for other kinds of loans.

While the lack of a U.S. Social Security Number (SSN), which is granted to U.S. citizens and legal residents, will make it difficult, if not impossible, to build a U.S. credit record or, for instance, obtain U.S. credit cards, there are lenders who will consider non-U.S. borrowers and will look at their overall financial picture in their decision-making.

One piece of misadvice commonly handed out is that the Individual Tax Identification Number (ITIN), which the IRS issues to non-U.S. taxpayers following an extensive application process, can substitute for an SSN. While the two types of numbers look alike, by law the ITIN can only be used for the singular purpose of filing federal income taxes. It is not legal to use it for any other purpose.

A basic point with which you should be aware is whether you are dealing directly with a given lender or through a loan broker. You also need to be aware whether any fees you are asked to pay are application fees, broker fees, or fees payable to some thind party, like a property appraiser, and whether or not they will be payable or refundable dependent on the success of your loan application or if they are retained regardless of success. Knowing these things in advance are important points to know and can avoid big surprises later.

If you are applying for finance in connection with a property purchase, be sure to have a finance contingency included in the sales agreement that will allow a reasonable time for the finance to be approved and which allows you to cancel the contract without penalty if you don't receive the finance.

Institutional Borrowing

This is borrowing from an established financial institution or lender. The range might include everything from a bank to a finance company or group to financial institutions that specialize in non-U.S. borrowers.

While most U.S. banks will not lend to non-U.S. borrowers, there are some that will consider it, and there are financial companies that do as well. Just as with the process of opening bank accounts can vary from bank to bank, so do their lending policies and requirements.

It is often the case that an institutional lender will impose additional requirements on a non-U.S. borrower than they will on an American buyer. These might include a minimum lending limit – ranging from well under $100,000 to the millions of dollars – and numbers of properties that must be included under a loan, higher interest rates, and stricter loan-to-value (LTV) requirements. Loans in the 60-to-75% LTV range are common for non-U.S. borrowers. Often portfolios of properties can be grouped together to meet the minimum loan requirements.

Most institutional lenders will require an appraisal of any properties to be borrowed against, and the borrower will usually pay the appraisal costs (about $300 to $500 for most single-dwelling units). What an appraiser says a property is worth may differ considerably from what you paid for the property or what you think it should be worth. Lenders also usually have a loan initiation fee that might be as little as $1,000 or up to some percentage of the loan amount.

Additionally, many lenders, including institutional lenders, will require the principals behind entities such as LLCs or corporations to take personal responsibility for mortgage loans. They also may have specific requirements on how property ownership or entity management needs to be structured. Often this means the individual borrower, not an entity like a trust or company, needs to be at the top of the ownership structure. Sometimes a local manager is required.

Taking personal responsibility for a property loan should not adversely affect the other asset-protection and liability-limiting benefits of operating and holding properties through entities such as LLCs or corporations. But changing the ownership structure potentially has both asset-protection and taxation implications and needs to be evaluated carefully. And some lenders require that all properties subject to a loan be put in the name of a single LLC. This can seriously impinge on the asset-protection aspect of spreading properties between several LLCs.

Other Lending Sources

Beyond institutional sources, there are other sources the non-U.S. investor may be able to borrow from. These include private money lenders and hard money lenders (these are two different kinds of lenders, and later in this chapter we will discuss how the non-U.S. investor can become a private money lender).

Normally these kinds of lenders will consider short-term loans, often at high or very high interest rates, and usually tied to a specific project for rehabbing or otherwise upgrading a property in preparation for re-selling or "flipping" it.

The private money lender is usually an ordinary person who has access to enough funds to lend out to investors at interest rates generally ranging from 8 to about 12 percent, often for terms between six months and two years.

The private money lender might be a professional person with a good income, like a doctor, dentist, or attorney, or it could be someone who has a fair amount of money salted away in retirement funds but who wishes to receive higher rates of returns. These lenders will look for security on their loans, normally obtained by being granted the first lien position on a given property.

Hard money lenders are usually people or groups who specialize in making loans to people who have difficulty obtaining the funds they need from other sources.

The credit standard applied by hard money lenders normally can be expected to be higher than that of private money lenders, as will be their interest rates. Hard money lenders will expect anywhere from 15 to 35 to 50 percent returns. I have even heard of 100 percent rates for some purposes and have been told "you'd be surprised" how many people accept this rate (aside: I was surprised!)

While both private money lenders and hard money lenders may consider lending to non-U.S. borrowers, since their loans are usually tied to a given project and property, involving a U.S. party as a loan broker, joint-venture partner, or introducer sometimes will assist in the process.

Seller Finance

Seller finance remains a tried-and-true way of financing a given acquisition. Even through the economic downturn, many sellers have been willing to take back mortgages in order to sell their properties.

This can be viewed as low-hanging fruit for the non-U.S. investor to pick. While not every seller will entertain offering to finance a part of the deal, it does not hurt to ask the question. Obviously, with deals presented as "cash sale only," this is usually not a likely possibility.

It is a rule of thumb that often the trade off for a seller to offer finance is that of price. The buyer gives the seller the price sought, and sometimes even a premium, if the seller agrees to take back a mortgage loan on the property. The interest rate paid on a seller-financed loan usually is a bit higher, too.

In cases where a buyer obtains a first mortgage on a given property a seller might be reluctant to take back a second mortgage. This puts the seller in a very precarious position in that a default on the first loan may result in a foreclosure in which nothing is left over to cover junior lien holders. While this was not always a problem in a world of rapidly rising property values, in today's environment of low- or no-growth values it becomes very risky.

A seller may be induced to be the sole lien holder, however, which gives him or her the security of being in the first-place position in the event of a default by the buyer.

Buying "Subject To"

Assumable loans used to be very common. One could buy a property and obtain an assignment to take over an existing mortgage on the property. Some types of mortgages were mandated to be assumable, often with no qualifying. This is no longer the case, and most mortgages today are not assumable by the buyer.

There are, however, ways of buying properties "subject to" an existing non-assumable mortgage. While it is beyond the scope of this guide to delve into the details of how this can be accomplished, keep in mind that most "non-assumable" clauses are triggered by registering the transfer of title on a given property.

Also keep in mind that, from sellers' perspectives, they want to know that a mortgage in their name is going to be paid properly, while lenders want to know that any arrears are settled and payments are made in a timely way. When deals are structured to accommodate these three basic points, it is often possible to acquire properties "subject to."

Joint Ventures

Another approach to obtaining finance is to form a joint venture with an American JV partner. There are different ways of structuring such JVs and divvying up shares.

There are lots of reasons to form a JV, but in the instant case of finance these can work in cases where the non-U.S. investor has cash but can't get credit, and a U.S. partner who may or may not have cash, but is eligible to apply for finance.

Often these JVs are structured in the form of an LLC with both partners members in the project LLC, either directly or, preferably, through their own entities. Again, clarity of terms, including what the partners are responsible for and an exit strategy for how the deal will be wound up and the partners get their funds out at the end, is very important.

Neither a Borrower Nor a Lender Be . . . But Wait!

While old Billy Shakespeare might have known of what he wrote on some levels, it is clear he was not a real estate investor. Any real estate investor can recite the benefits of being a borrower. But what about being a lender?

In truth, most real estate investors don't even consider the benefits of lending their funds rather than acquiring properties with them. But that's what we're going to look at in this sub-section: Becoming a private money lender, and why.

Picture the following:

- Returns on investment in the 8-to-12% range or higher – guaranteed by prior arrangement

- Quick turn-around on your funds: Just 6-to-24 months in most cases

- Full securitization of your funds in a first lien-holder position

- None of the hassles of being a property owner or landlord

- No vacancies

- No problematic property managers

- No troublesome tenants

- No rental arrears

- No risk of property depreciation

- Limited currency conversion risk

Sound good? Well, it's not too good to be true. It is the reality of being a private money lender.

In considering private money lending, make sure you have the basics in place, including a written agreement signed between you and the borrower, a full repayment schedule, including any monthly payments and balloon payments to be made at the end of the loan term, and placement of a mortgage lien in the first position (and *only* the first position) on the property involved.

You should ask for details on how the borrower plans to use your funds and plans to make payments, and of course there is no substitute for doing reasonable due diligence on the borrower, project, and property.

So you can see from this brief overview that there may in fact be several finance options open to you as an overseas investor, and even a way for you to become a lender yourself.

---

1 http://www.scoreinfo.org/overview-of-fico-scores/fico-score-basics/

Other Considerations

There are several other things you, as a property investor in the U.S., need to be aware of and to take care in. Some of the bigger issues are covered in this chapter. This is by no means a comprehensive treatment of all ongoing or other considerations, but it does touch on the ones many, if not all, investors will need to confront.

Pricing When Buying and Selling

One of the biggest challenges facing the real estate investor is how much to pay for a property when buying and how much to ask when selling. These are critical challenges and can make a huge difference in how well the investor does in the long run.

As I've pointed out, you make your money when you buy, not when you sell, a property. That might sound like a contradiction, but consider that when you buy you're not only setting the benchmark against which your selling price will compare or contrast, but you're also determining how much return you can earn through rentals, how hard it will be to attract and keep good tenants, what kinds of repairs or maintenance you'll incur, and what other issues, such as crime and vandalism, you may encounter.

Don't just take an offering price at face value. It's all too easy to overpay for properties and you'll be stuck with that factor as long as you own the property. The same goes when selling. Don't just accept what an agent tells you the property is worth. Do your own analysis, or ask for it to be done and verify that it was done right. That analysis is based on comparables – what other similar properties in the area or equivalent areas have sold for recently (not last year or three months ago).

As an investor, you want to make money and that means you want to pay as much under market value as possible. And when selling, be aware that other investors will be trying to do the same and are likely to offer considerably less than either market value or what a prospective occupant-buyer might offer.

One rule of thumb that experienced investors apply is that the purchase price, plus the cost of repairs or rehab, plus any holding costs (such as interest on a protracted rehab), should not exceed 70% of the after repair value (ARV, determined by analysis of comparables) of the property. That gives you some margin for error and still allows you to come out ahead.

Other Key Details When Buying

There are some other things to be aware of when buying. Ideally you should actually see and inspect the property before you contract to buy it. In any case, you should have a thorough inspection of the property performed by a qualified home inspector (you'll pay for this, and usually the cost runs about $200 - $400 per unit). And be sure to have a contingency included in any sales contract that allows you reasonable time to have the inspection done and that specifies the parameters either for the seller to pay for any repairs needed (usually up to a given amount) or for you to cancel the contract without penalty or loss of your deposit.

If you're applying for finance, as noted in the "Finance" chapter, be sure there is a finance contingency allowing reasonable time for loan approval in the sales contract. And as noted, generally the lender will require an appraisal to determine how much the source will lend against the property.

When a property requires significant repairs or rehab that the seller or a third party undertakes to complete, be sure to get any commitments in writing, including details of the work to be done, the costs of the work and who pays them, a given schedule or deadline when the work is to be completed, any penalties that apply if the work is not completed on time, and who bears the cost of lost rent due to delay in completing the work.

Another thing to be aware of is that part of what you're paying may be going to agent commissions and possibly finder's fees. Some of these costs will appear on the closing statement (what is called the HUD-1), but some may be hidden and subject to side agreement. While agents and other intermediaries are entitled to fair compensation, I have heard of some truly outrageous finder's fees way out of line with the value of the properties, grossly inflating the prices the buyers paid. So do watch for this and don't be afraid to ask if you sense the price is out of line. Or just walk away.

Property Management

You're probably going to be thousands of miles away from your U.S. rental properties, so having good property management in place is of utmost importance.

Perhaps the biggest complaint we've heard from our overseas clients concerns poor property management. We've seen everything from negligence, with municipal and homeowner association violations allowed to occur, to inattention to damage inflicted by tenants, to excessive vacancy rates caused by failure to keep a property rented, to property managers actually absconding, taking clients' funds with them.

There is more to picking a good property manager than representations made by the manager or third parties, and certainly far more than the rate they charge. Some of the biggest property management failures we've seen were with managers recommended by third parties who had a vested interest in closing deals. Do your own due diligence, seek recommendations from other investors you trust in that market, keep a close eye on whatever property manager you select, and be prepared to change managers when necessary.

As for rates, these can vary greatly. Usually there will be an upfront fee, such as the first month's rental, and then ongoing charges are based on a percentage of the rental amount. In general these range from 6-to-10%. Paying a higher rate does not necessarily guarantee that you will get better service, just as a lower rate does not mean you'll get shoddy service. We've heard raves – good and bad – at both ends of the spectrum.

If you plan to own and rent out a vacation property, with occupancies ranging from as short as a week up to a month, you'll want to have a manager who specializes in short-term rentals and who is prepared to take care of such details as unit cleaning and preparation, checking renters in and out, and related services. The rate for such service is likely to be higher than that charged by a standard property manager.

As with any agreement, read property management contracts carefully. Can you get out of the contract if you're unhappy with the service, or any other reason? Or will you be stuck for a full year? What is expected of the property manager? Who pays what expenses? What things, like regular property inspections, are expected of the property manager?

In most states, property managers are covered by state real estate licensing laws. That means a manager must hold the appropriate license, and is held to certain legal and ethical standards. Failure to meet those standards can allow you to file a complaint with the state licensing board. But consider that if things get to that point you've already experienced serious problems, and the remedies open to you and the cost and hassle of pursuing them may be inadequate to resolve your issues or recover your losses. Still, the threat of an official complaint might spur a recalcitrant property manager into action.

Stay informed, stay on top of things, demand reasonable compensation for your losses if they are the result of the agent's negligence, and don't delay to make your concerns known to your property manager if you begin to see warning signs that things are not being handled as they should be.

Perhaps the biggest problem any landlord must deal with is the tenant who falls behind in rent, or who simply refuses to pay. Your leases should have clear statements of the tenant's responsibilities, and don't wait for a tenant to fall so far behind that your profit is essentially wiped out. Sob stories are a dime a dozen, and some tenants will play on your sensitivities and string you along as long as they can. But if you apply your reason to things, what are the chances, realistically, that a tenant a month behind in the rent is going to ever catch up on arrears and stay current, even if they sincerely intend to do so? Add to that the time it takes in most jurisdictions to evict a non-paying tenant, and you begin to see why delay is not on your side. Nor should you be tolerant of a property manager who permits such delays without taking action on your behalf.

A non-paying tenant also can do significant damage to your property, and you will quickly find that the security deposit you're holding doesn't cover a fraction of the cost of the damages caused. So your management agent should exercise great care in selecting and doing background checks on tenants. While no one wants properties to go vacant, taking the first applicant who walks through the door just to fill your vacancy is not looking after your best interests.

Some of these things might seem self-evident, but still people wind up putting themselves in a bind on a disturbingly regular basis. Often people let their hearts – or their willingness to trust others, or their enthusiasm, or whatever – rule over their heads, and sad stories and the accompanying losses often are the result.

Two other things you need to be aware of. First, some property-owner insurance policies provide coverage for lost rents. While such coverage might add a bit to your premiums, it could be well worth the cost. And some lenders require such coverage. Second, and this applies especially in lower-income areas and lower-grade properties, there is a government program known as Section 8. Under Section 8, the government, usually in the form of a housing authority, subsidizes the rent paid by the tenant. Again, while this might help get your property rented, you have to consider the quality of tenant you might get and there have been some unhappy results to landlords with Section 8 tenants. Again, you have to weigh the advantages and disadvantages of going this route.

On another side of things, with properties in areas with large military populations, there might be a Department of Defense program that will cover your rents when renting to a service person who is unexpectedly transferred. Local real estate agents are usually aware of such programs and can help guide you when purchasing.

Lease-to-Own, Land Contracts, and Other Potential Pitfalls

There are some other considerations that the investor needs to be aware of. We've seen clients misled on some of these points, and in general there are seemingly subtle points to be aware of to avoid problems.

First of all, there is a distinct difference between a lease-to-own arrangement and what is commonly known as a land contract. In the former case, a tenant leases a property and puts down a deposit toward possibly purchasing the property at some point down the road. If done properly, the tenant remains a tenant and has no ownership interest in the property until such time as the tenant opts to put the purchase agreement into action.

In the case of a land contract, a tenant gains an ownership interest in the property from the very beginning, and a portion of the rent paid is attributed to the ultimate purchase of the property at a pre-set price and time.

While these may seem to be similar arrangements, and sometimes are presented as such, there are important legal and practical differences between them. In fact, some states have outlawed land contracts due to abuses, and others have put significant restrictions on them.

Be sure, when presented with any kind of arrangement where the tenant would ostensibly be purchasing the property, to know what the arrangement is, check out the relevant state law, and be sure to structure things properly.

From the investor's point of view, the biggest problem comes from giving a tenant an ownership interest in the property being leased. Depending on the state and legal restrictions, a tenant can claim to be an owner of the property and the only way a landlord can get rid of such a tenant in the event of non-payment or other malfeasance is to file a foreclosure against the tenant.

Especially in what are called "judicial" foreclosure states – states where a court action is necessary to foreclose on a property – this can be an expensive and time-consuming process, in some cases stretching not just into months, but into years. And there are (to use a polite term) "professional tenants" who know exactly how to work the judicial process to their advantage to remain in a property while paying nothing to the landlord.

Without an ownership interest, a non-paying tenant is subject to eviction. As messy and inconvenient as eviction can be, it is a far easier and less difficult process than a foreclosure.

An investor might want to enter into a lease-to-own arrangement with a tenant for various reasons. For one thing, it can liberate the landlord from having to provide repairs and upgrades on the property, transferring those responsibilities to the tenant. And ostensibly a tenant who plans to buy a property will take better care of it than one with no long-term interest in the property. The investor also has some expectation either that the property eventually will be sold at a given price, or else there will be a sum of liquidated damages that go to the landlord, and the whole process can be re-initiated.

In a lease-to-own arrangement, the key is to keep rental and ownership interests separate. Two documents are necessary: A lease, which makes no mention of the lease-to-own arrangement, and a buy-sell agreement that sets out terms of the sale.

Under the first document, the tenant is a renter and does not obtain any ownership interest in the property. Meanwhile, the second document is put into trust with an attorney, title company, or other fiduciary agent who holds the buy-sell agreement along with the deposit (usually a substantial amount – say, for instance, $10,000 – to secure the seller's interests that a sale may actually take place and to demonstrate the buyer's sincere interest in buying the property).

No part of that deposit must ever touch the seller's hands until such time as the buyer either acts to implement the purchase of the property or defaults under the lease and the buy-sell agreement. Then and only then does the deposit go to the seller, either as a part of the down payment on sale of the property or as liquidated damages in the event of a default by the tenant/buyer.

The reason for this is that the investor does not want to give any ownership interest to the tenant until such time as the tenant decides to implement the buy-sell agreement. If the tenant subsequently defaults, the landlord can enter an eviction against the tenant and does not have to go through a foreclosure which otherwise might be required to remove the tenant were the tenant to gain any ownership interest in the property.

These may seem like trivial distinctions, but they are actually important legal points and help protect the investor from potentially costly and troublesome complications. Obviously, you are advised to consult an attorney or other professional familiar with the proper structuring of lease-to-buy arrangements and not simply depend on the representations of sellers or agents.

Whether dealing with property managers, sellers, agents, or tenants, two Latin words should always apply: *Caveat emptor.* Buyer beware.

Taxes, Taxes, and Taxes

It is said that two things are inevitable: Death and taxes. The former is above our pay grade and beyond the scope of this book, so we'll confine ourselves to the latter.

In the U.S., there are three levels of taxation: Federal, state, and local. Overseas investors tend to focus on the first level and are often in a bit of a quandary when it comes to the other two levels.

Taxation is a subject onto itself and is covered in the next chapter ("Tax Matters") of this book.

Tax Matters

If it is any consolation, U.S. taxation remains a mystery to most Americans. So if it baffles you as a non-American, don't feel somehow deficient.

I have long believed that there should be a proper name for the mental illness that clearly afflicts those who draft the federal tax code, not to mention the myriad maze of state tax codes.

Making matters even worse is the inconsistency with which the rules and regulations are interpreted and the misinformation that regularly is given out by the Internal Revenue Service (IRS) and state tax agencies. Surveys taken over many years repeatedly show significant erroneous information given out to taxpayers by IRS employees in response to tax questions. Even doing their best to put things in a positive light, government surveys show that barely 60 percent of U.S. Taxpayers have a positive or mostly positive view of the IRS, that figure dropping to barely half of of those in the 50-plus age group.[1]

Making matters worse still, the IRS web site, irs.gov, was ranked in 2014 as the most frustrating government web site by users, hands-down beating out the hugely problem-plagued healthcare.gov.[2]

Even airlines, the source of much customer irritation, ranked ahead of the IRS in customer satisfaction in 2014.[3]

As someone who deals regularly with the IRS, I would say that correct information and proper interpretation of the rules is more the exception than the rule in dealing with the agency and, if anything, things are headed in the wrong direction. So if you think you've been
led astray by the IRS, you might well have been. And none of this is encouraging in a country that depends so much on voluntary taxpayer compliance with tax laws.

Now that we've put things in perspective of the reality, what do you need to know about U.S.

taxation? Let's break it down in a systematic way, starting with a brief discussion of the types and levels of taxation to which you might be subject.

Of course, none of this is intended as specific tax advice, and you need to engage a competent tax adviser familiar with U.S. taxation, and especially taxation as it applies to LLCs and corporations, which has its own set of complications. And most likely an adviser familiar with taxation in your home country, too, to be sure you remain within the bounds of tax laws and regulations and file your taxes and pay neither more nor less than the legitimate amount of taxes you owe to various jurisdictions.

Types of taxes: Income taxes

In the U.S., there are several types of taxes. Starting at the top, there is federal personal income tax and its business equivalent, federal corporate or business income tax. And note that the U.S. has the third highest top marginal corporate tax rate of any country in the world. Federal taxes are paid on income earned on a personal or business basis, and may also cover such things as capital gains, inheritances, and other related items included in the tax code.

Note as well that some expenses, such as acquisition and major rehab costs, are considered capital expenses and go to what is considered the "basis" of a given property. The basis is used to determine the extent of any capital gain or loss when the property is later sold. Depreciation claimed as a deduction on the property annually also is "recaptured" at the time of future sale and is subtracted from the basis. How these things are treated under U.S. tax law may be different from how your home country treats them.

While one factor cited as a drawback of corporate tax treatment is dual taxation, first of the corporation and then of any dividends it pays out to shareholders, corporate tax treatment actually can be advantageous over personal tax rates for the first $50,000 of net income (income after all deductions). Given that a corporation does not have to pay out dividends and when dividends are paid out they do not carry self-employment tax obligation, corporate tax treatment can be beneficial. With real estate, however, the downside comes on sale of an owned property since corporate capital gains rates are higher than the personal rate. Again, look at all the factors in deciding the structure and tax treatment you opt for.

If you do hold a corporation, something to be aware of is IRS Form 5472. This is the form filed by corporations – as well as by LLCs that elect to be treated as corporations for tax purposes, but not other LLCs – owned 25 percent or more by foreign shareholders. The downside for failing to file this form is a $10,000 penalty, unless you qualify for one of several exemptions in the filing requirements. At least one of my clients was hit with this penalty, so if you have a corporation or LLC treated as a corporation as part of your investment structure you, as a non-U.S. investor, need to be aware of this form and the need to file it or qualify for a filing exemption.

If you have a trust at the top of your ownership structure, you need to be aware of U.S. tax regulations and rates that apply to trusts. The trust tax rates are extremely high – the top rate is the same as the corporate top rate, but it's reached at just over $12,000 in net income. But with certain specific types of trusts, notably pass-through trusts or trusts where the income is passed through or distributed to the beneficiaries on a non-discretionary basis, the income is then claimed by the beneficiaries at lower personal tax rates. Again, do your research and consult with someone familiar with tax laws as they apply to overseas trusts to see what works – or doesn't – for you.

Beyond federal taxes, there are state taxes. Most, but not all, states also have either or both personal and business income taxes. Some states also have what are called franchise taxes which are assessed on businesses for the right to do business in those states. They have nothing to do with business franchises, such as owning, say, a McDonald's or Super 8 Motel, but pertain to the "franchise" or right to operate in the state. State and local taxes can add significantly to your tax bite and are a factor to include in evaluating where you plan to acquire investment properties.

Of the 50 states plus the District of Columbia, seven have no state personal income tax, and two don't tax wage income. The first seven without personal income tax are Alaska, Florida, Nevada, South Dakota, Texas, Washington State, and Wyoming. The remaining two states – New

Hampshire and Tennessee – don't tax wages, but they do tax interest and dividend income.

Just three states – Nevada, South Dakota, and Wyoming – don't tax businesses, while three states – Ohio, Texas, and Washington State – impose a gross receipts or franchise tax on businesses rather than a business income tax, though in some cases these may not impact the small investor.

For instance, Texas's franchise tax doesn't kick in (at this writing) until $1,110,000 in gross receipts, though a franchise tax report must be filed annually even if no tax is owed. Note that some states have both business income and gross receipts or franchise taxes. So much for "free" enterprise, so touted in the U.S.

If these taxes are not enough, some counties and cities also impose their own personal and business taxes. In higher-tax jurisdictions, it is not uncommon to pay more in taxes than one keeps.

Property Taxes

Beyond personal and business income taxes, there are two other general kinds of taxes employed in the U.S. of which the real estate investor needs to be aware. These are property taxes, assessed against real property and, in many states and locales, personal or business property as well, and state sales or excise taxes.

One downside of non-existent or very low state income taxation is that often government – this is normally municipal or county governments, or special taxation districts – will resort to higher property taxes to compensate for the lack of income on one side and to generate it on the other.

Again, one example of this is Texas, which has some of the highest property tax rates in the country. If it is any compensation, some states that have every sort of personal and business taxation also have high property tax rates. An example of such a state is my home state of New Jersey, as well as neighboring New York.

As a property owner, you need to be aware of what property taxes will be assessed against your holdings, and by what taxing jurisdictions or districts. You also need to be aware of when tax bills are issued in the jurisdiction or jurisdictions where your properties are located, and these can vary throughout the year in various jurisdictions.

Many jurisdictions will offer a small discount for early payment of property taxes, a period when the actual amount is due, and then penalties are added to any outstanding amounts. Failure to pay property taxes in a timely way will normally trigger a series of warnings, and then at some point – depending on the state and locale – the taxing jurisdiction will take the action allowed by law in the state where your property is located.

In some cases, your outstanding taxes might be sold off at auction, in which case you will be required to pay the successful bidder not only the back taxes but a significant interest rate on what is owed. Or in some cases a more dire approach might apply, and the taxing jurisdiction can foreclose on your property and sell it off at auction to pay the taxes. You may or may not be eligible for any overage generated, depending on the state, and you may (or in many cases will not) have a right to recover the property from the successful bidder.

Similar provisions may apply to assessments made by homeowner or property owner associations. In any event, property taxes and special district and association assessments are not to be trifled with.

You may receive correspondence about applying for a homestead exemption, or you may see such an exemption applied to your property tax bill. The homestead exemption is employed in many states to give homeowners a reduced tax rate as well as some protection against attachments of their property by creditors.

Note that you must live in a given property and it must be your primary residence (not a part-time or vacation home) to qualify for a homestead exemption. If you don't meet those minimum requirements, you are not eligible for a homestead exemption. Be aware of homestead exemptions when a property seller shows you a tax bill, or tells you the taxes paid on the property, to be sure you determine the full tax bill you'll be paying on the property, without the homestead exemption.

There is normally a process for appealing a tax assessment on your property. You may or may not win such an appeal, but some of my clients have succeeded with their appeals and had assessments reduced.

Sales or Excise Taxes

Finally, the last major form of taxation that is commonly employed is what are generally referred to as sales taxes. The U.S. does not employ a Value Added Tax (VAT) as many countries do, but most states do tax retail sales of many goods and, in some cases, services.

When these taxes are paid on business property – for instance, say when you need to purchase a new heating unit or new carpeting for your real property – you normally would be able to deduct the full amount of the purchase, including the sales tax, as a business expense against your personal or business income taxes, though such deductions between states may be limited.

In addition to state-level sales taxes, there also may be local or county sales tax add-ons.

Five states – Alaska, Delaware, Montana, New Hampshire, and Oregon – either assess no sales taxes, or allow limited local sales taxes or only assess sales taxes on limited items, such as restaurant meals or lodging.

Note that some states may call their sales taxes, either in general or on certain items, excise taxes (there also are federal excise taxes on some items), and while a sales tax on a high-ticket item, such as a car, bought in one state may be deductible in a second state at the time of registration, a sales tax might not be deductible in a state with an excise tax, or vice versa.

How do I know this? I once had to pay sales tax on a vehicle I bought in Florida and was assured the sales tax would be deductible when I registered the vehicle in Maryland, where I was living at the time. But Maryland calls its tax on vehicles an excise tax and would not allow the deduction of sales tax paid in Florida. Florida would not refund the sales tax I paid, so I wound up paying tax twice on the same vehicle. What a deal!

Bilateral Tax and Investment Treaties

As if all this is not confusing enough, there is the whole question of bilateral tax treaties that the U.S. has signed with a number of countries around the world. These treaties, in simplest terms, are intended to reduce or eliminate dual taxation between what the taxpayer may owe in federal (and sometimes state) taxes in the U.S. and also what is owed in his or her home country.

A list of countries with tax treaties with the U.S., and their provisions, can be seen here:

http://www.irs.gov/Businesses/International-Businesses/United-States-Income-Tax-Treaties---A-to-Z

Here is a list of countries with investment treaties with the U.S., and the dates they came into effect:

http://www.state.gov/e/eb/ifd/bit/117402.htm

Tax and investment treaties and their application present complex questions beyond the scope of this book, and a good tax adviser familiar with how to apply a tax treaty between the U.S. and your country, or a visa adviser familiar with investment treaties, would be a good choice to help you negotiate these tricky areas of law and regulation.

As you can see from this brief overview, taxation has many moving parts, and to maximize your profits and reduce your tax bite, you need to look at all of them.

I go back to one of the earliest admonishments I offered in this book: It is not how much you bring in, it is how much you keep, that matters. Taxes are one of the biggest sponges on what you bring in, so limiting your tax bite should be a critical element of your investment strategy.

While you don't want to give up to high-priced consultants what you save on the tax side, striking the right balance is one of the biggest challenges you will face as an investor. I wish you well in this, and in all elements of your investment activity.

I hope the guidance offered in this book assists you in your efforts and helps you navigate, or at least better understand, the sometimes tricky waters of investing and doing business in the U.S.

---

1 http://www.treasury.gov/IRSOB/reports/Documents/IRSOB Taxpayer Attitude Survey 2014.pdf

2 http://fcw.com/articles/2014/11/07/news-in-brief-november-7.aspx

3 http://www.usatoday.com/story/travel/flights/2014/04/22/airlines-have-low customer-satisfaction/7976785/

Looking Forward

We've covered the basics of setting up your U.S. investment structure, asset-protection, and some of the contingencies of doing business in the U.S. What you ultimately do is up to you and the professional advice you receive and implement, but this book should serve as a brief and ostensibly helpful primer for you.

Now we'll take a look at some of the broader things you need to be aware of as you go forward. It is easy to put things on autopilot and forget or neglect your investment enterprise, and ignore changing conditions, and this is often when trouble takes root.

It's also easy to get set in a certain mode of operation and not look at other alternative approaches. Something, of course, can be said for the old adage, "If it ain't broke, don't fix it." But an environment of changing market and economic conditions might quickly overwhelm your position and gains.

The Bigger Picture

On the micro level, market changes can wipe you out. On the macro level, we see how literally trillions of dollars were lost in the major financial debacle of 2008-09. Many investors, homeowners, shareholders, and other stakeholders were devastated by what transpired in the course of several crucial months and the following period, which to some extent still continues.

It drives me to distraction when I hear such drivel – often put forth by so-called "gurus" and "pundits" defending their own negligence and incompetence – that "no one could have seen this coming."

Really? Unless one was living in a cave on Okinawa for the prior 60-some years, the warning signs were all writ large, and anyone observing and heeding them would have seen it coming. All the signs of a growing and accelerating bubble, especially in the housing market, in an environment where virtually all the fundamentals were lacking, were there for anyone who cared to look.

I am a big believer in what are considered economic and fiscal fundamentals: Low or non-existent fiscal deficits, low and controllable levels of consumer debt, reasonable market appreciation, diversified investment, low inflation, and rising levels of real productivity, being some of the key indicators. Applying them I was able to foresee the 2008-09 meltdown several years in advance, as well as most of the major financial dislocations, both in the U.S. and overseas, of the two decades that preceded it. These can be good guidelines for you to apply, too, as you look at market prognoses, whether in the U.S. or anywhere else.

At this moment, one can argue that several key indicators remain pointed in the wrong direction in the U.S. economy, as well as in several other economies. There are lots of predictions of impending doom floating about. But there also are countervailing conditions at work, such as the Federal Reserve keeping the stock market more buoyant than it otherwise ought to be through its policies of quantitative easing (QE) (still being used by several other central banks) and low interest rates. A goodly share of the financial sector is in better overall shape now than it was in 2008. And much of the rest of the world, especially Europe, looks even worse, so all this tends to continue to drive investment to the U.S.

On balance, I am not quite ready to jump on the doomsday wagon. Not to say that another financial collapse is not possible, but for now I don't see this as an imminent probability (define "imminent" any way you like – I just can't make a firm prediction at this point with any kind of reasonably realistic time line behind it).

The overseas investor clearly is faced with mixed messages, though. On the one hand, the recently surging U.S. dollar has made it a lot more expensive, in the investor's domestic currency terms, to buy into the U.S. On the other hand, anyone already invested here probably finds their capital gains and income magnified by shifts favoring the U.S. dollar *vis-a-vis* their home currency.

On the market level, there was a surge in hedge funds buying up foreclosed and otherwise vacant properties in some metro areas. This drove up market prices in those cities, again mitigating against the new investor while favoring the property values of those already invested. But it also put a lot of new inventory on the rental markets, making rentals more problematic. And then when some hedge funds found themselves saddled with a lot of non-performing properties, this then put new downward pressure on market prices, a process again reversing in some markets. Meanwhile, many home buyers are locked out of the buying market because they can't get finance, keeping them in rentals.

What's the main point of this admittedly long-winded discussion? Simple: It is imperative that investors continue to watch economic and fiscal conditions both on the national and macro levels, as well as in the specific markets where they are invested or are considering. What was correct yesterday might not be correct today. What is correct today may be very incorrect tomorrow.

Do your own observation and analysis. There are lots of so-called investment advisers, property vendors, "gurus," and "pundits" who will offer you bogus advice from which they might profit but which will offer you little or no value. And be cautious of promises of very high returns. Remember the two tried-and-true premises of any investment: The higher the potential returns, the greater the risk. And if it seems to be too good to be true, it very likely is.

To reiterate a term used earlier in this book: *Caveat emptor! Semper!* Always!

Keep in mind as well that it is possible to make money on both a rising and a falling market. But one must know the rules and methods for dealing with each, and they are often mutually exclusive.

Investment Alternatives

It's worthwhile to be open to investment alternatives. It's beyond the scope of this book to delve into all these, but here is a short list. Some may already be in your plans and others are worth considering:

- Buying and holding single-family rental houses or duplexes

- Investing in apartment buildings and complexes

- Investing in commercial properties, such as shopping centers and office buildings

- Investing in income properties such as storage units, parking facilities, and mobile home parks

- Investing in vacant or agricultural land

- Flipping properties – buying and rehabbing or re-positioning them, or buying low and selling high

- Employing a strategy that has a mix of "flips" (for short-term gains and growth) and buy-and-hold properties (for long-term income)

- Investing in joint venture pools which acquire larger or multiple properties, spreading the risk both across holdings and participants

- Investing in both performing and non-performing loans (yes, non-performing loans can be profitable)

- Investing in tax certificates and participating in tax auctions

- Helping property owners obtain funds to which they are due but may be unaware (such as overages in tax foreclosure sales)

- Private-money lending (covered in more detail in the chapter on "Finance")

- Investing in Real Estate Investment Trusts (REITs)

All these various ways of investing involve real estate, though obviously there are other investment modalities, too. And the same structures, guidelines, and advice outlined in this book can be applied to many of these investment alternatives.

Best wishes for your success!

It's been fun recounting what I have in this short guide. There is a practical benefit, too, in that I figure it also will undoubtedly save me lots of time answering the same questions multiple times.

Further to that end, I'm also including some of the more common questions, with their answers, in the FAQ section in the after pages of this guide. And the Glossary will help explain many key terms to you, too.

One thing I hope I was able to convey is that none of this is rocket science. Just about anyone with reasonable diligence and care and funds to invest (and in some cases, not even much of those) can invest in the U.S. and have a good chance at success. Careful selection of investments, knowing how to navigate the ins and outs, and staying on top of things are the keys.

I am accessible to your questions and ideas, so I hope you will feel free to contact me with those. I also hope you will allow me to assist you with setting up or expanding your U.S. investment venture.

Whatever you do, I wish you all the best for your success, and hope that, in some small way, I have been able to contribute to it.

FAQs

This section is intended to provide quick answers to some of the most common questions asked about the process of investing in the U.S. It is by no means intended to be comprehensive, and your specific questions might not all be presented or answered here.

You will find more detail in the text of this book and, when appropriate, you should seek professional guidance to obtain the specific answers you require.

Q: Do I need an attorney to set up an entity?
A: No, in most cases you don't. The registration process is straightforward and we can accomplish that for you. While you can even do this yourself, you

need to be aware of some special conditions or requirements of some states and would need to seek out your own registered (statutory) agent. We can accomplish all this for you for much less than an attorney would charge you, and help you avoid any pitfalls. Additionally, you have several options for drawing up your operating agreement or bylaws and other papers. We can assist you with that as well, and we are always happy to explain your options.

Q: Do I need a separate entity for each property I own?

A: This really depends on the nature of the properties and the liability profile you are willing to carry. In general, the liability coverage provided by your property-owner insurance is your first line of defense in the event of a lawsuit. While some people prefer to put each single-family residence into the name of a separate entity, others will put two, three, or even more single-family residences into a single entity. Another approach is to set a dollar limit on holding more than one property in a single LLC to limit the asset value at risk. Again, that depends largely on the liability profile you care to maintain. If, however, you are holding multifamily residences, such as apartment buildings or complexes, or commercial properties, my recommendation is to hold each of those under a separate entity due to the much higher liability profile of such properties.

Q: Do I need to register in each state where I hold rental properties?
A: While simple property ownership by an entity does not normally require registration in any state (though it does in California), collecting rent from a property normally changes the legal environment and in most states this then requires registration. Some states spell out this requirement in their statutes, but most simply say "and nothing more" other than simple property ownership does not require registration. Therefore, collecting rents is considered doing business and requires registration. In any case, in all states, regardless of the registration requirement, an entity can be sued whether it is registered in the state or not, but the entity will be barred from filing suit if it is not registered in the state. So, for instance, the entity will not be allowed to file for eviction or collection of back rents or other damages if it is not

registered in the state. My recommendation is that if you are holding rental properties in a state you should register in that state, either as a domestic (in-state) entity or foreign (out-of-state) entity.

Q: If I register in a state with top asset-protection laws, like Wyoming, Nevada, or Delaware, will the same protections apply when I register or do business in another state?

A: There is no cut-and-dried answer to this question. Much depends on judicial discretion – what any given court or judge will decide – and the facts of a given case. Legal precedent also varies from state to state. In general, many courts will refer back to the parent entity as member or owner of the child entity, so if the parent entity is, say, a Wyoming entity, and the child entity in the other state is owned by that entity, the courts may be more likely to defer to Wyoming law. However, if the parent entity registers as a foreign (out-of-state) entity in the other state, and does not register a new child entity owned by the Wyoming entity, it is agreeing to submit to the laws of the other state. A court in that case might more likely apply that state's law to the entity. Again, there is no clear answer that applies in all cases in all states to this question. But being registered initially in a state with top asset-protection laws is more likely to enhance an entity's asset protection and would not harm it.

Q: What is a registered agent? Do I need one?
A: All states require that an entity registered in that state, either as a domestic or foreign entity, maintain a registered office or agent in the state. Some states allow a company or company principal or manager to serve as registered agent, but they still require a street address (often a commercial street address) in the state to be listed. Other states require that entities have a specially designated registered agent (also called a statutory agent in some states). Unless you have access to an acceptable representative and address in a given state that permits self-representation, you will need to employ a registered/statutory agent when you register your entity in any state. While many people confuse the purpose of the registered/statutory agent as someone who will act on your company's behalf for various purposes, the sole purpose of the registered/statutory agent is to be of record should your company be

presented with legal papers or service. The agent will then pass those papers or service on to you. The registered/statutory agent has no other role and you should not ask or expect the agent to perform other services on behalf of your company. Some agents offer optional services, but they charge additionally for those services so you should expect to pay for them if you retain the agent to perform other optional services.

Q: Do I need an address in the U.S.?
A: For lots of reasons you'll find a U.S. address very useful. Whether for banking purposes, insurance documents and billing, corresponding with property managers or other representatives, or receiving other personal or business correspondence or parcels, a U.S. address will be most useful to you. This should be a street address and not a post office box. Our company offers a U.S. commercial street address at a very reasonable cost, supported by personal service, that almost all our overseas clients make use of. This is a low-profile address that won't trigger banking alerts, as many of the bigger mail centers will. Some banks will not open accounts if the address triggers a

banking alert that the address is a mail center. You also may find a U.S. phone number, readily available through a number of services, useful, both for communication purposes as well as for completing various forms, some of which only accept U.S.-format phone numbers.

Q: Do I need an EIN for my company?

A: You will find that doing just about anything, from purchasing property, opening a bank account, setting up property management or insurance, or filing taxes, among other purposes, requires an Employer Identification Number (EIN). While the EIN of a parent entity can be used for child entities, it is most convenient when each entity has its own EIN. This also would apply to opening separate bank accounts for the entities.

Q: How do I apply for an EIN for my company?

A: If you do not already have a U.S. Taxpayer Identification Number (SSN, ITIN, or EIN), you will need to apply initially for an EIN by fax. You also can file a paper application (IRS Form SS-4 is used for this purpose, whether by fax or on paper), but it can take weeks to obtain the EIN by paper filing. Theoretically, the IRS will provide an EIN in response to a faxed application in four business days, but often this is not done or the IRS asks for additional information. It may be necessary to call the IRS to free up an EIN or see what the problem is. Once an initial EIN is obtained, normally EINs for companies downstream from the parent company in the same ownership chain can be obtained online on the IRS web site and usually the number is issued instantly. The problem is that there is little predictability to what the IRS will do or decide, or what works in any given case.

Q: Will you apply for an EIN for my company?
A: After numerous problems in dealing with the IRS, and expending countless hours trying to unravel them, at present we are no longer filing initial EIN applications for clients. We will complete the Form SS-4 for clients for a fee that the client will then fax or mail themselves to the IRS. Once the initial EIN is obtained, at present we will apply for downstream EINs, for a fee. Some registered agents also will either complete the Form SS-4 or file the EIN

application for clients, but they have their own fees and processes for doing so.

Q: Will you apply for an ITIN for me?

A: Applying for an ITIN is a relatively complex process that requires submission of specific documents to the IRS. I do not get involved with this process. You can make this application yourself, and there also are designated ITIN agents in some countries that are authorized to handle ITIN applications for individuals. Consult the IRS web site for more information on this topic.

Q: Can an ITIN substitute for an SSN?

A: No. Under federal law and regulation, the sole purpose of an ITIN is to enable non-American taxpayers without an SSN to file their federal tax returns. Any other use is illegal. While some people attempt to use ITINs to apply for credit, this is an illegal use of the number and most credit-granting institutions (not all, and not in all cases) require an SSN on credit applications, and credit reporting records and scores are based on individuals' SSNs.

Q: Do I need an operating agreement for my LLC or bylaws for my corporation?

A: While most states do not require them, it is very useful to have in place an operating agreement for an LLC or bylaws for a corporation. This would apply even in cases of single-member LLCs or single-shareholder corporations. For one thing, it's a sign that you are operating your company as an entity separate from yourself and not just as an extension of yourself, or as your personal piggy bank. Importantly, an operating agreement also lays out who (or what entity) owns the LLC, the processes for how the company will be governed and operated, whether an LLC is member- or manager-managed, how to take in new members, voting rights and how profits will be distributed, and how to transfer or dissolve the company. Corporate bylaws lay out shareholder rights, how the company will be directed, when and how meetings will be held, and other key elements. Many closing agents, banks, and others will ask for these documents, and in some states they are required to do so. Additionally, the ancillary documents that often accompany these documents, such as initial meeting minutes, will contain important resolutions granting contracting authority, signatory authority for banking (often referred to as a "banking resolution"), naming officers, setting any salaries or other compensation, and other key company functions.

Q: What is a charging order, anyway?

A: Many states provide that a successful litigant or creditor can only use a charging order to obtain compensation under a judgment. States such as Wyoming with especially good asset-protection laws set this out by statute, and not just judicial precedent, and apply the rule to both single- and multi-member LLCs and partnerships. In simple terms, a charging order permits compensation solely from the distributions paid out to the members of an LLC or partners of a limited partnership. No attachment of personal property of the member or members is permitted, nor is taking of the property of the entity permitted (not to be confused with barring taking of property under a foreclosure on that property), nor any claims on other entities held by the member or members. There is no obligation for the entity to pay out distributions, and so a creditor may be left with no

132

recourse. Often a settlement between the creditor and debtor organization is the outcome of a stalemate. Note that these protections only apply to actions committed by the entity (inside liability) and not to actions committed as individuals by the members or partners (outside liability). However, by putting real estate holdings in a limited liability entity, this takes them out of the individual's name and can shield them in the event of a lawsuit entailing outside liability. See the chapter of this book on "What State(s)" for more information on charging orders.

Q: What about a single-member LLC? Can a creditor take it over?

A: In some states a single-member LLC is vulnerable to a take-over by a successful creditor or other litigant. This is one advantage of a registration in a state with top asset-protection laws, such as Wyoming, which specifically bar such take-overs and offer protections for single-member LLCs as well as multi-member LLCs. If this possibility exists in a state where you register an entity, one way to potentially avoid such a possibility is to add a second member, perhaps a spouse or trusted business partner, and provide that person with a small percentage of ownership in the LLC if they are not actively involved in the business. If you have concerns about this issue, seek legal guidance on how best to structure your company and ownership.

Q: Should I have a separate bank account for each of my entities? Why?

A: See the chapter on "Banking" in this book for more detailed responses to these questions. The short answer is, yes, you should. And there are at least two main reasons as to why you should. The first pertains to asset-protection: You don't want to give a successful litigant or creditor access to all your funds in one shot by having just one account for all your entities. The second is a more mundane reason in that many banks now are refusing to accept third-party checks (checks made payable to one entity but signed over for deposit to another).

Q: Will I have to make a personal appearance to open a U.S. bank account either for myself of my entities?

A: The bad news is that, in most cases, you will. And the worse news is that some banks even will require subsequent personal appearances to open accounts for new companies you set up. The banks use the USA Freedom Act (the replacement for the former U.S. Patriot Act) as their reason for this requirement, even though the act says they must know their customer. This does not necessarily translate to a personal appearance requirement – much less so once a customer has already appeared and has done business with that bank – but most banks cover themselves with the personal appearance requirement. See the "Banking" chapter of this book for more details.

Q: Can I set any fiscal closing date I wish for my company, such as my country's closing date?

A: It depends. Corporations normally can set any closing month they determine, as can an LLC that elects to be taxed as a corporation. The closing month for an LLC otherwise normally is the same as the closing month for the member or members of the company. However, if the member or members of an LLC are individuals and not entities, then the default U.S. tax year for individuals applies. That is the calendar year that runs from January 1 to December 31.

Q: Are there any things I should know if I decide to register a corporation versus an LLC?

A: Corporations and limited liability companies are not the same and are subject to different tax treatments, different tax filing dates, and also may have different entity filing requirements (dates, costs, and requirements) in various states. For instance, the corporate tax filing date is the 15th day of the third month following the close of the corporation's tax year, but for individuals and some other entities, it is the 15th day of the fourth month following close of the tax year. Corporations and LLCs taxed as corporations that are held 25% or more by foreign shareholders must file IRS Form 5472 with their tax returns or face a $10,000 penalty, unless they qualify for a specific exemption. Capital gains taxes also are different for corporations than for individuals. There also is a possibility that an individual who is a shareholder in a corporation can have their shares foreclosed on by a successful litigant. See the chapters on "Structure" and "Tax Matters" of this book for more information.

Q: What is a series LLC? Should I form one to hold multiple properties?

A: A series LLC is a form, currently permitted by 15 states, the District of Columbia, and Puerto Rico, in which several LLCs ("series LLCs") can be formed under one structure and filing. While series LLCs are presented as an effective way of holding multiple properties in separate LLCs, there are both advantages and disadvantages to the series LLC form, and it is not a form we recommend going into lightly. It is often more expensive to form a series LLC than a standard LLC, but ongoing expenses are usually less, both in terms of annual fees and registered agent fees, since usually a single registered agent is required for the series. On the negative side, laws vary from state-to-state and there is not a lot of jurisprudence on series LLCs, so how a series LLC is treated in one state might be very different from how it is treated in another state. This can affect liability protection, taxation, and other factors. Each LLC in the series should be operated as a separate entity, which reduces some of the financial benefit to be gained by the form. Additionally, some states allow registration of foreign (out-of-state) series LLCs and some don't. It's important to weigh the advantages and disadvantages of series LLCs in light of one's objectives before deciding on this form.

Q: My property manager has absconded, taking my funds with him/her. What can I do?
A: You have a big problem, don't you? The time to address this problem is before you retain any property manager. Make sure a property manager has proper state-required licenses. Ask to see them, and if you have doubts, verify that the licenses are current and in good standing with the state real estate licensing body in that state. Ask for references. Check the references. Don't just accept the referral of a seller or wholesaler, who has a vested interest in getting a quick sale from you. Read over the management contract carefully to see what your rights and responsibilities are, as well as those of the manager. See what the cancellation terms are. If you sign an

agreement and start to see lengthy vacancies, delayed rent collections, or notices of violations from municipal bodies or homeowners associations, these are clear signs your property manager is falling down on the job. If the manager stops sending you your rents, don't wait six months to react. Even one missed payment is a sure sign that something is very wrong, and you need to take immediate action. As more than a few of my clients have learned, once a property manager has absconded there is little that can be done. Filing suit or filing a complaint with the real estate licensing board might or might not provide any satisfaction.

Q: Should I buy to rent and hold, or should I buy to flip the property?

A: The answer to this question goes back to the objectives and strategies you lay out for yourself. Refer to the chapter on "Basics and Objectives" on this question. In general, if you are looking to build your capital, you might want to look into buying, upgrading, and flipping properties. If you are looking for long-term income, you would more likely look to buying and holding, generating income through rentals or other means geared toward income generation. A balanced approach might combine these two approaches, with a certain number of flips used to build capital combined with some buy-and-holds to build long-term income. Note that holding a property for less than a year subjects any profits made on its sale to short-term capital gains tax treatment, which is less advantageous than long-term capital gains treatment. But that might be acceptable under your specific investment strategy. You do, however, need to take steps to qualify as an investor and not be deemed by the IRS to be a dealer in properties. Further research on what qualifies for dealer status is worth the trouble since a dealer incurs a much higher tax rate. Again, taking a good look at your situation, resources, and goals, and planning and implementing a strategy based on that examination is the starting point.

Q: Are there any other questions I should ask?
A: If you don't understand something, and you can't find a satisfactory answer from your research or in this book, you should ask. The time to find out something is before you wind up twisted up in your

own shoelaces or in some other sort of difficulty. I am always ready to address questions within my purview, and more complex tax and legal questions should be directed to professionals knowledgeable in those areas. I won't burden you with the old cliché that the only stupid question is the one you don't ask, but you get the point. You do, don't you?

Glossary

After Repair Value – The fair market value of a property after any needed repairs or rehabilitation is completed.

ARV – After Repair Value.

Annual Report – A report filed by a corporation, limited liability company, registered partnership, or other business entity required by some states of entities registered in that state; sometimes reports are required biennially, diennially, or at other intervals, and normally a fee is associated with filing the annual (or other) report.

Articles of Formation – The term used by some states for Articles of Organization (see "Articles of Organization").

Articles of Incorporation – The statement of facts and other required information that establishes a corporation.

Articles of Organization – The statement of facts and other required information that establishes a limited liability company.

Backup Withholding – Backup withholding is applied by a taxing body, such as the IRS or a state taxation authority, on certain kinds of income – notably interest, dividends, rents, royalties, commissions, non-employee compensation, and other payments including broker proceeds – when a correct taxpayer identification number and required forms are not supplied. The federal backup withholding tax rate currently is 28%. Backup withholding does not affect the actual tax due in the end, though a tax return will need to be filed to determine the actual tax due, and it will delay access to any excess tax withheld.

Banking Resolution – A resolution passed by a corporation, limited liability company, or other entity that authorizes one or more individuals to set up bank accounts and serve as signatories on the accounts on behalf of the entity.

Basis – The original acquisition cost of a property, including rehab costs, less claimed depreciation, that is used to determine gains or losses for tax purposes.

Bilateral Tax Treaty – A treaty between the U.S. (in this case) and another country providing for special tax treatment or reciprocity for taxpayers subject to both countries' tax laws.

Bilateral Investment Treaty – A treaty between the U.S. (in this case) and another country providing for special treatment or reciprocity for investors from one country within the jurisdiction of the other.

Bylaws – The covenants governing the operation of a corporation.

"C" Corporation – An IRS tax designation of a corporation under which the corporation is taxable as an entity and then dividends paid out to shareholders are taxable again at rates applicable to the shareholders; all U.S. corporations are by default "C" corporations unless they elect for "S" corporation tax status.

Capital Expense – The acquisition cost of a property and an expense that materially adds to the value of the property, prolongs its life, or adopts the property to a different use.

Capital Gain or Loss – The difference between the sale price of a property or security and its basis, less claimed depreciation.

Certificate of Authority – A certificate or permission issued to an out-of-state corporation, limited liability company, or other business entity granting the authority for that entity to operate and do business in that state.

Certificate of Good Standing – A certificate, sometimes called a Certificate of Subsistence or other name, issued by a state certifying that a given entity is currently registered, has met all filing requirements, and otherwise is in good standing with that. state.

Closing – When the title of a property passes from one party to another and all details of the transfer, including loans and payments, are brought to closure and final settlement.

Closing Agent – The agent who handles a closing.

Commercial Property – A property having non-residential, i.e., business, purposes; term also includes apartment buildings or complexes with more than four rental units.

Corporation – A specific type of company structure created under state statute which provides limited liability protection to the shareholders.

Credit Score – A scale for rating a person's deemed creditworthiness issued by the three major credit reporting companies and the Fair Isaac Corporation; different scales and rating factors are used by all the various companies.

Deed – The document that provides title and proof of ownership to a property.

Deed-in-Lieu-of-Foreclosure – When a property owner returns the deed and ownership of a property to a lender in lieu of the lender filing for a foreclosure on the property.

Deed of Trust – What a mortgage is termed in a non-judicial or trust state (see "Non-Judicial State").

Default – Failure to meet the requirements of a loan or contract.

Director – A person responsible for overall oversight and setting of policy of a corporation; a director may or may not be an officer of the corporation (see "Officer").

Domestic Entity – In this context, an entity registered in its home, or "domestic," state.

EIN – Employer Identification Number.

Employer Identification Number – A type of taxpayer identification number issued by the IRS to companies, sole proprietorships, trusts, and other organizations and associations.

FICO® Score – Fair Isaac Corporation credit score.

Flipping – Buying a property and reselling it at a profit either by rehabbing and upgrading it, repositioning it in the market, or simply by buying low and selling high.

Foreclosure – An action taken by a lender, lien holder, or a taxing body against a property for non-payment, respectively, of a loan, lien, or taxes by the owner or owners of that property.

Foreclosure Sale – Sale of a property, usually at auction, under a foreclosure action.

Foreign Entity – In this context, an entity registered in another, or "foreign," state or country.

Franchise Tax – A tax some states impose on companies for the right (or "franchise") to operate in those states.

Hard Money Lending – Private lending, usually at high interest rates and for short terms, when other sources of borrowing are either unavailable or too time-consuming or difficult to obtain.

HUD-1 – A form of the federal Department of Housing and Urban Development (HUD) used by a settlement or closing agent itemizing all charges assigned to a buyer, borrower, and seller in a real estate transaction. This form gives a picture of the closing transaction, and provides each party with a complete list of incoming and outgoing funds. Also known as a closing statement.

Incorporator – A person who incorporates a corporation; an incorporator has no rights over or responsibilities for the entity formed once it is registered by the state.

Individual Taxpayer Identification Number – A type of taxpayer identification number issued by the IRS to non-resident individuals who do not qualify for a Social Security Number for the sole purpose of filing federal income taxes.

Inside Liability – The liability incurred by an entity through the acts of that entity (see also "Outside Liability").

IRS – Internal Revenue Service.

Internal Revenue Service – The U.S. federal agency responsible for interpreting and enforcing federal tax law and regulation and collecting federal personal and business income and other taxes.

ITIN – Individual Taxpayer Identification Number.

Judicial State – A state in which a lender must go into court and obtain a court judgment to foreclose on a property; foreclosures normally take much more time to execute in such states than in non-judicial states.

Land Contract – A specific kind of document, not permitted in all states and strictly limited and defined in others, in which a prospective buyer is acquiring a property over time, with a set purchase price and payment terms normally stated in the contract.

Lease-to-Own – An arrangement wherein a tenant leases a property and signs a separate document indicating the intent to purchase the property at a future date; the lease and purchase are, or should be, separate processes, and a lease-to-own arrangement is different from a land contract.

Legal Person – Entities such as corporations and LLCs are usually recognized as legal persons with certain rights and responsibilities that might otherwise pertain to human persons.

Leverage – The use of borrowed funds or financial instruments to increase the potential return of an investment.

Lien – A claim placed against a property by a creditor, taxing authority, homeowner association, or service provider that allows the lien holder to sell the property or to enforce its interest at time of sale of the property to collect the amount owed by the property owner.

Limited Liability Company – A company structure created under state statute that provides limited liability protection to the members (owners); a limited liability company is not a corporation and, unless it elects to be taxed as a corporation or association, it is not taxed as an entity but rather taxes are passed through to the member or members.

Limited Liability Partnership – An entity that operates much like a limited partnership, but gives each member of the entity protection from personal liability, except to the extent of their investment in the entity.

LLC – Limited liability company.

150

LLP – Limited liability partnership.

Loan to Value – The amount a lender is willing to lend against a property as a percentage of the appraised or market value of the property.

LTV – Loan to Value.

Manager – In the context of an LLC, this term carries a distinct legal connotation; an LLC manager may be an individual or an entity; see "Member-Managed LLC" and "Manager-Managed LLC" for more clarification of the term.

Manager-Managed LLC – An LLC that is managed by an outside manager that is not a member of the company; this is a distinctly different management structure from the member-managed LLC; that a company is manager-managed, as well as the name of the manager, must be declared in states that require an LLC to state how it is managed, and these points of information should be included in the company operating agreement.

Mechanic's Lien – A lien placed against a property by a service provider, such as a contractor (see "Lien").

Member – An owner of an LLC; a member may be an individual or an entity.

Member-Managed LLC – An LLC that is managed by its members; this is the default assumed by most states that do not require an LLC to state how it is managed, and management by the members should be stated in the company operating agreement; most states do not recognize a "managing member" of a member-managed LLC but assume all members are responsible for management of the company.

Mortgage – A loan obligation "given" by a property owner (mortgagor) to a lender ("mortgagee"), who "takes back" the mortgage, in which the property on which the loan is taken is held out as collateral for repayment of the loan; mortgages can be in first (senior) or second or lower (junior) lien positions on the property (see "Lien").

Non-Judicial State – A state (also called a Trust State) in which a lender can foreclose on a property without the requirement of going into court and obtaining a court judgment; normally a mortgage (or "deed of trust") in such states names a trustee who acts on the lender's behalf; some states allow both judicial and non-judicial mortgages and foreclosure processes.

Non-Performing Loan – A loan on which the debtor has stopped making payments.

NPL – Non-Performing Loan.

Officer – A person responsible for the day-to-day running of a corporation or LLC, or some aspect thereof; officer titles include President, Vice President, Treasurer, and Secretary; most states allow one person to fill all, or multiple, officer positions; not to be confused with the legal term "Manager" of an LLC (see "Manager").

Operating Agreement – The agreement between the members that governs the operation, management, dissolution, and other processes of a limited liability company; while not usually legally required, it is a good idea for an LLC to have one.

Organizer – A person who organizes or forms an LLC; an organizer has no rights over or responsibilities for the entity formed once it is registered by the state.

Outside Liability – The liability incurred by the members or partners of a limited-liability entity, through their acts as individuals; liability protections granted to limited-liability entities normally do not extend to outside liability (see also "Inside Liability").

Performing Loan – A loan in which the borrower is making payments in a timely and correct way.

Private Money Lending – Private lending done by private parties normally at higher-than-market interest rates, usually for shorter terms, and tied to a specific property or project, with the private money lender usually holding a lien on the property (see "Lien").

Property Manager – An individual or company charged with managing properties belonging to others; property managers are required to be licensed in most states.

Real Estate Investment Trust – A type of security that invests in real estate through property or mortgages and often trades on major exchanges like a stock. REITs provide investors with a liquid stake in real estate and receive special tax considerations and typically offer high dividend yields.

REIT – Real estate investment trust.

Real Estate License – A license issued by a state agency granting the right to act within that state as a real estate broker, broker-salesman, salesman, appraiser, or property manager.

Registered Agent – A person or company, required in all states, designated to be of record for a corporation, limited liability company, registered partnership, or other entity, to receive legal service for the entity; called a statutory agent in some states.

RLLP – Registered limited liability partnership.

"S" Corporation – An IRS tax designation of a corporation under which corporate income is passed through to the shareholders and is taxable to the shareholders at rates applicable to them; a corporation must elect "S" corporation status, non-U.S. parties cannot be shareholders of an "S" corporation, and shareholders are limited to 75.

Series LLC – A series LLC is a form, currently permitted by 15 states, the District of Columbia, and Puerto Rico, in which several LLCs ("series LLCs") can be formed under one structure and filing. While series LLCs are presented as an effective way of holding multiple properties in separate LLCs, there are both advantages and disadvantages to the series LLC form. See the discussion of Series LLCs in the FAQs section of this book.

Settlement Agent – Closing agent.

Shares – The ownership fractions of a corporation; shares may have special categories (i.e., common or preferred), may be designated voting or non-voting, and may be assigned a specific value or termed "no par value," which indicates the shares have no set value, or have floating value; also called a corporation's stock.

Shareholder – An individual or entity that has an ownership interest in a corporation; also may be known as a stockholder; a shareholder may or may not also be a director or officer of the corporation.

Short Sale – Sale of a property in which a lender agrees to accept less than the amount outstanding on a mortgage as the sale price.

Social Security Number – A type of taxpayer identification number issued by the IRS to individuals, including U.S. citizens, legal permanent residents, and other U.S. residents, who have a legitimate right to remain in and, unless otherwise indicated, to work in the country.

SSN – Social Security Number.

Statutory Agent – A term used by some states for a registered agent (see "Registered Agent").

Stock – See "Shares."

Stockholder – See "Shareholder."

Tax Certificate – A certificate issued by a government body to a successful bidder who pays an outstanding tax on a property in return for compensation by the property owner at a given rate of interest if and when the property owner redeems the tax certificate.

Tax Lien – A lien put by a government body on a property for failure to pay property or other taxes (see "Lien").

TIN – Tax Identification Number; this can be a Social Security Number, Individual Tax Identification Number, or Employer Identification Number.

Trust Deed – See "Deed of Trust."

Trust State – See "Non-Judicial State."

Underwater – When the market value of a property is less than the amount owing in mortgages or liens on it.

My Services

I've been setting up entities – primarily corporations and LLCs – for more than a decade. First were my own companies and organizations, and for the past several years those of my clients. Additionally, I've been conducting business within entities for something like 40 years.

From my perspective, I am hard-pressed to think of any serious pursuit, profit or non-profit, that should not be conducted within an entity. Prime advantages are outlined in detail within this guide, and they include asset protection, tax, and image and professional benefits.

At this juncture, I've registered or provided corporate services to hundreds of companies in about half of the 50 U.S. states, as well as in some other countries, and the number continues to rise. I've learned more than a few things as a result of this experience, and continue to.

The first thing I've learned is that each state and country has its own stated requirements, as well as a set of what I would classify as unstated idiosyncrasies or process specifics. This is where experience comes in and has great value. It also comes in when determining how one structures and operates one's entities.

To be perfectly honest, almost anyone can register a company in most jurisdictions, and certainly in most, if not all, U.S. states. The relative ease with which this can be done is one of the advantages of doing business in the U.S. One can read the rules, complete the forms, and write a check or enter credit card information. But that is only part of the story, part of the process.

The rest of the story, of the process, is that element of experience, doing things repeatedly, getting to know those aforementioned idiosyncrasies and process specifics, and years of research, questioning, comparing, and information gathering.

And knowing how to handle things following the initial registration.

I don't mind saying that these elements of experience and knowledge embody the real value of my services. And I price my services so that virtually anyone can find them affordable and a good value.

It is said that it is better to learn from the mistakes of others than from one's own mistakes. I'll take that a step further: It is better not to make any mistakes at all from which to learn, and just get it right in the first place.

Okay, enough verbiage. Here are the primary corporate services I offer at present:

- Company registrations in any U.S. state and many off-shore jurisdictions
- Setting up registered agent service in any U.S. state and many off-shore jurisdictions
- Transfer of existing registered agent services
- Preparation of initial company documents – corporate bylaws, LLC operating agreements, initial meeting minutes, waivers of notice
- Preparation of annual company documents

- Provision of corporate/LLC kits

- Assistance with Employer Identification Number applications

- On-going consultation to assist with basic company questions

- Guidance in how best to structure ownership to meet individual objectives

- Provision of a U.S. commercial street address, scanning, and forwarding service that clients can use for all their business and personal mail

- Mail deposit of checks to U.S. bank accounts

- Referral to practical U.S. telephone services

- Referral to high-value, cost-effective legal, accounting, tax preparation, and property management business services

  Upon urging by many loyal clients, I'm also now offering these financial and real estate services:

- Referrals and broker services to providers of finance to overseas real estate investors

- Referral to an international currency exchange and transfer service offering economical transfers between numerous world currencies

- Marketing-partner assistance to help clients market their U.S. properties offered for sale

- Identifying good deals for real estate flips and buy-and-holds

- Setting up or facilitating joint ventures to acquire and upgrade properties, obtain finance, and flip or hold properties

- Intermittently being able to assist clients open U.S. bank accounts without personal visits

- Assisting with residence visa applications, including EB-5 (international immigrant investor) visas, and identifying and setting up suitable investments

- Identifying and offering good real estate deals in other countries, whether for investment, vacation, retirement, or a combination thereof

I also am available for domestic and overseas speaking engagements and seminars, as well as publishing, on topics related to corporate structure, asset protection, and real estate acquisition, upgrading, and sales, and a number of other topics. Private consultation on these topics also is available.

Please feel free to inquire with me:

frank@alphaopportunities.com

And visit our company web sites:

alphabiz.us

alphaopportunities.com

Acknowledgments & Reviews

I'd like to express my sincere gratitude to the many clients, professional associates, and friends who read and commented on this book. Their assistance and suggestions have been invaluable.

I'd especially like to acknowledge the professional contributions of Lisa Boucher, Sean Adams, and Ed Corrigan, who offered their professional views on the information in the book as it relates especially to tax, finance, and banking issues, respectively.

Lisa and Sean kindly offered to provide professional reviews of the book, and those reviews are provided here.

Professional Reviews

In *Buying America the Right Way* Frank Yacenda gives some great advice on investing in properties in the U.S. The book is well written and very easy to understand. Frank gives examples of ways to structure the ownership of such properties and how these examples can be used in different situations.

Frank also comments on the complex tax issues that occur with these investments, and what can happen if you do not file correctly or ignore various tax liabilities. He also, unashamedly, tells his readers that he is not a tax expert and that he has had dealings with the IRS that in some cases did not go well. Investing in U.S. properties is not as daunting as some might make it seem, and this book proves that.

Lisa Boucher, EA, Greenback Expat Tax Services, Greater Boston, Massachusetts, USA

In *Buying America the Right Way* Frank Yacenda highlights right at the beginning that it is not how much money your investments make that

165

matters, it is how much you get to keep. This book covers the potential pitfalls of not looking carefully into how you own your U.S. property, and highlights that if not done correctly, you will find that you are potentially losing out on the value of your investments.

In easy to understand language Frank explains the ownership structures and how their set up varies from state to state. He explores the intricacies of the more popular structures and touches on the processes and complications encountered when considering everything from bank accounts, funding, and registration fees to filing accounts and dealing with registered agents and property managers.

In summary, this book is an essential starting point when deciding how to protect your future asset purchases.

**Sean Adams, International Director,
SPF Private Clients, London, UK**

Testimonials

Frank's knowledge and assistance in getting my U.S. business and entities in place have provided a welcome relief. The mine field of legislation and hoops to jump through have been dramatically simplified through his experience. I have found Frank's willingness to assist, his ongoing support, affordability, and his level of service a cut above the rest.

Having a street address was one of the best pieces of advice for a relatively small fee, for without it it's nearly impossible to fill out forms. I've also found it cheaper to use my U.S. address when purchasing online for delivery costs and that some companies simply don't accept overseas delivery when shopping online.

I can't recommend him enough for anyone wishing to purchase property or setup a business in the USA.

Andrew Thomas, Investor, New South Wales, Australia

Frank Yacenda is undoubtedly the best contact person I have in the United States. His knowledge and understanding of a very complex U.S. system is invaluable and I would have saved myself hundreds of dollars and avoided many of the problems and pitfalls I encountered if I had taken advantage of Frank's services earlier.

I love the fact that I am free to use some or multiple services and his responses to any questions or queries are always answered in a timely manner. Frank has a very simple, logical approach to any problems and charges a fair and very reasonable rate for his services.

Nothing I could write – no matter how many pages of praise and compliments I could put together – would do justice to the way I feel about your ongoing help and support. No matter how many testimonials, I could never repay you for your help and kindness.

Anne Trounson, Investor, Victoria, Australia

Since we met him, Frank has been a very reliable person, always available with a prompt answer to explain and support us in the different steps of our

LLCs' formation. We are very satisfied with the services he offers.

In his book you find all those suggestions that come from experience and that you need in order to have successful investments. You are guided in detail in those technical aspects that can be easy if you know, but can turn into big problems when you don't.

Matteo Gallini & Sabine Mannequin, Investors, Swieqi, Malta

Frank Yacenda has been the best support I could have possibly asked for when undertaking the huge venture of buying property in the U.S. Living and working in Australia, understanding the different complexities involved in the set up of my structures was a challenge for me. Without Frank I would have made any number of mistakes, and most likely not be in the excellent position I am today. I have no hesitation in recommending Frank's book, or his services, to any person looking for a full and ongoing service provider for your entities and mail in the U.S. His attention to detail is outstanding. You will not be disappointed.

Monica van Riet, Investor, Victoria, Australia

If you felt lost when it comes to successful real estate investment in the US, this book will not only show you the correct way, but will also give you good guidance to avoid myriads of traps.

Apares Chakrabarti, Investor, Victoria, Australia, and Kolkata, India

I have read your book and am in awe of your ability to have captured so succinctly all the requirements for offshore purchasers of U.S. residential property. If only a guide such as this was available when Carol (with my oversight) was purchasing her properties.

Noel Stone, Free-Lance Editor, Queensland, Australia

I read the book on my flight to Brisbane as I said would and was absolutely delighted with it. To say that it is long overdue is a massive understatement and the book hits all the right points in exactly the right way. It is not overly complex and laden with jargon and it is not too technical, and neither is it too low or simple.

The explanations are precise and clear and sufficiently thorough without being confusing. The content is perfect in every respect and it suits a global market. I would have no hesitation in recommending this book to anyone considering investing in the U.S.

The assistance, advice, guidance, support and friendship provided by the author has been an immeasurable benefit to so many investors over so many years. I have the utmost confidence in the author and the information contained in the book and recommend his services without reservation.

John Bone, Investor and Investment Adviser and Software Developer, Victoria, Australia

I wish I had read this book before investing! I was very very lucky to find you – you have been a great mentor and have always pointed me in the right direction. And thanks to you, my asset protection is properly in place.

Rory Gordon, Investor, Victoria, Australia

Excellent book on investing in real estate in the United States. Frank is an expert on protecting your real estate purchases and property investment strategies. I wish I had read this book before I started investing in the U.S. I found it very informative.

Dean Woodward, Investor, New South Wales, Australia

This book is informative and so pertinent for those of us known as 'Foreign Aliens' taking the first steps to investing in real estate in the USA. I am very impressed with its accurate relevance to the journey I have taken and it has covered all the scenarios I was confronted with.

Frank was, and still is, of immeasurable assistance when negotiating the minefield of U.S. regulatory authorities. Since 2012 when I embarked on the purchasing of U.S. properties from my home base in

Australia I ran into the myriad of unknown rules that must be undertaken to complete these purchases. Frank, as affable then as now, guided me through this raft of regulations and still does to this very day. His assistance is prompt, easy to understand and, most importantly, reliable. A Guiding Angel for those of us dealing with a very different set of corporate rules, from our familiar home country.

This guide is something I would have cherished at the time but I could always rely on Frank to give me the correct, and timely, information to complete my purchase, as well as ongoing and reminder support in meeting U.S. annual reporting obligations. I have no hesitation in recommending this book and/or Frank to any proposed purchaser of U.S. property, and indeed anyone who requires assistance with undertaking any kind of business in the USA.

Carol Rogerson, Investor, Queensland, Australia

Being a complete beginner in the world of international property investing, I had the extreme good fortune to be introduced to Frank through a mutual connection. From outlining best practices (none of which were available in a book such as this at the time) in terms of U.S. business structures and state-specific business nuances, through to actively managing the creation of my property investing business structures, I truly believe Frank has provided me with the means to succeed in this game.

Frank's knowledge of U.S. business registrations is first-rate. That, combined with a tremendous amount of energy, ensured I was able to get my U.S. investment vehicle off the ground in a matter of days.

Lastly, I am confident that Frank's experience and the way he will provide not only specific information relating to, for example, which U.S. state to incorporate in, but also examples and links to relevant information, has lead me to make a success of my U.S. investing endeavours.

Robert D. Parvin, Technology Executive and Investor, Victoria, Australia

I first heard of Frank about four years ago when I started investing in the USA. A friend recommended his services for establishing companies. At this point Frank has created five companies for me in the U.S. and another two elsewhere. His services have always been of the best quality, his mail forwarding service is outstanding, and his advice is priceless.

I am happy and proud that Frank shared his book with me. It is very well worth reading carefully from start to finish. Thanks, Frank, for doing an excellent job!

Witold Dudkiewicz, Investor, Warsaw, Poland

About the Author

Frank Yacenda has had an international outlook his entire life, beginning as a child setting up pen pals for classmates and crossing the Atlantic and Pacific by ship.

Since 2010, he has been setting up U.S. companies for overseas real estate investors. In between he was a diplomat with the U.S. Department of State, served a range of international clients in his award-winning public relations and advertising firm, worked as a journalist and science writer covering U.S. and European space programs, and lived, worked, and traveled in 70-some countries around the globe.

Combining this international perspective with decades of business and real estate experience makes him the ideal guide for his many overseas clients and, not coincidentally, the author of this book.

Credits for Cover Images

Aspiration Clouds courtesy of gratisography.com and pexels.com

Suburban Street with Big Clouds by Margan Zajdowicz, courtesy of freeimages.com

Small Neighborhood courtesy of bossfight.co

Retro Look At Palm Trees Against Clear Blue Sky by Ed Gregory, courtesy of stokpic.com

USA Map Badge by creative daw (salingpusa), courtesy of freeimages.com